Cambridge El

Elements in the Politics of Development
edited by
Melani Cammett
Harvard University

Ben Ross Schneider
Massachusetts Institute of Technology

 MIT CENTER FOR INTERNATIONAL STUDIES

UNDOCUMENTED NATIONALS

Between Statelessness and Citizenship

Wendy Hunter
University of Texas, Austin

 CAMBRIDGE
UNIVERSITY PRESS

CAMBRIDGE
UNIVERSITY PRESS

University Printing House, Cambridge CB2 8BS, United Kingdom

One Liberty Plaza, 20th Floor, New York, NY 10006, USA

477 Williamstown Road, Port Melbourne, VIC 3207, Australia

314–321, 3rd Floor, Plot 3, Splendor Forum, Jasola District Centre, New Delhi – 110025, India

79 Anson Road, #06–04/06, Singapore 079906

Cambridge University Press is part of the University of Cambridge.

It furthers the University's mission by disseminating knowledge in the pursuit of education, learning, and research at the highest international levels of excellence.

www.cambridge.org
Information on this title: www.cambridge.org/9781108701570
DOI: 10.1017/9781108568913

© Wendy Hunter 2019

First published 2019

A catalogue record for this publication is available from the British Library.

ISBN 978-1-108-70157-0 Paperback
ISSN 2515-1592 (print)
ISSN 2515-1606 (online)

Undocumented Nationals

Between Statelessness and Citizenship

Elements in the Politics of Development

DOI: 10.1017/9781108568913
First published online: July 2019

Wendy Hunter
University of Texas, Austin

Author for correspondence: Wendy Hunter, wendyhunter@austin.utexas.edu

Abstract: Understood simply, people are either citizens of a country or stateless. Yet reality belies this dichotomy. Between absolute statelessness and full citizenship exist millions of people who are nationals of a country in principle but lack the identity documents to prove it, beginning with a birth certificate. Languishing in a gray zone, undocumented nationals have difficulty accessing the full services and rights that their documented counterparts enjoy. Drawing on a range of country examples, *Undocumented Nationals: Between Statelessness and Citizenship* calls attention to and analyzes the plight of people who cannot exercise full citizenship owing to evidentiary deficiencies. The existing literature has not adequately conceptualized and examined this in-between status, which results sometimes from state neglect and other times from intentional state discrimination. By highlighting its causes and consequences, and exploring ways to address the problem, this Cambridge Element addresses an important gap in the literature.

Keywords: birth certificate, identity documents, statelessness, citizenship, undocumented

ISBNs: 9781108701570 (PB), 9781108568913 (OC)
ISSNs: 2515-1606 (online), 2515-1592 (print)

Contents

1 Introduction

Millions of people worldwide languish in a gray zone between full citizenship and total statelessness. Lacking the documentary proof to authenticate one's existence can blur the line between the two. Roughly ten to fifteen million people globally are now considered to be truly stateless, defined by international law as someone "who is not considered as a national by any state under the operation of its law"[1] and who has no "enforceable assertion" of a nationality.[2] However, a much larger number of people – an estimated 1.1 billion people worldwide – have a plausible claim to state membership through either birthplace (the principle of *jus soli*) or parentage (*jus sanguinis*) but cannot officially prove their identity (World Bank 2017). People who go through life without official papers that prove their citizenship typically did not have their birth registered or certified.[3] In most countries of the world, having one's birth entered into the civil registry is a vital step on the pathway toward full citizenship.[4] Lacking essential documentation is not simply a problem among older cohorts, some of whom were born before civil registries even came into existence in their countries; as recently as 2012, there were still roughly 750 million unregistered births globally among children under the age of sixteen years (Dunning *et al.* 2014: 2). One in every three new births in the world still is not registered in a timely fashion.[5]

Failures to register a birth among people who are, in principle, nationals of a country can result in untold deprivations, including some of the very same deprivations associated with full-on statelessness. Not having a birth certificate often bars a person from attending school or sitting exams, receiving health care (including immunizations) and social grants, opening a bank account, inheriting property, voting, and receiving burial assistance.[6] The difficulty in proving the age of unregistered/uncertified children puts them at increased risk of being subject to child labor (Fagernäs 2014), child marriage (Plan International & Coram International 2015), and underage military recruitment (Simmons 2009: 343). If elderly people cannot show evidence that they are old enough to be

---

[1] United Nations Convention relating to the Status of Stateless Persons, 1954, article 1(1).

[2] See Price (2013: 447).

[3] Birth registration is the official recording of a birth by the state in the civil registry of a country. Birth certification is an individual's formal proof that this has occurred. It is not unusual in the developing world to find people whose births were registered but who never received a birth certificate.

[4] Birth registration does not generally confer nationality per se. Instead, it establishes a legal record of where a child was born and who his or her parents are, information that is crucial for showing entitlement to nationality.

[5] For additional numbers on underregistration, see Gelb and Metz (2018: 44–45).

[6] In many countries, the absence of a death certificate precludes survivors from eligibility for funeral assistance and from burying the deceased individual in a legal cemetery.

eligible for a pension, they are vulnerable to income poverty (HelpAge International 2011). In part because it complicates the acquisition of subsequent identity documents (IDs), such as social security cards and passports, lacking a birth certificate excludes individuals from receiving and exercising the full benefits and rights that documented nationals enjoy (Hunter 2019). Proof of state membership not only helps one navigate within one's own country, but also is crucial for one to reach other countries and operate effectively abroad. Leaving a country that is beset with any number of problems (e.g. national disaster, war, famine, or even major unemployment) is impeded by not having the identity papers required to obtain a passport. In conflict situations, prior documentation greatly facilitates one's ability to reunite with family members. In short, proof of state membership, with all the downstream benefits it entails, begins with having one's birth documented.

Beyond the individual costs of nonregistration, there is a collective cost to having large segments of the population unincorporated into civil registration and vital statistics systems. The benefits of birth registration and certification extend beyond individuals to include the effective functioning, planning, and monitoring efforts of modern states. The lion's share of attention in the academic literature has focused on the surveillance and control-oriented aspects of why some states seek to make their populations legible (e.g. Scott 1998, Foucault 2007). It is true that countries headed by totalitarian regimes generally have profiles of near-universal registration. Indeed, objectives such as taxation, the control of movement in border regions and within the country, conscription, and internment rest on knowing the population. However, other compelling collective reasons exist for having fully functional registration and vital statistics systems, but these reasons are less recognized outside specific communities of experts. For example, it is impossible to arrive at an accurate statistical understanding of national epidemiological trends, such as infant mortality and life expectancy, in the absence of reliable vital statistics provided by a complete civil registry, which is why public health professionals have long been among the most consistent champions of birth registration in many developing countries (McGuire 2010). Moreover, everything from determining the number of schools to build to deciding on the number of vaccines to order rests on having an accurate count of the population (World Vision International 2014, Mikkelsen *et al.* 2015).

The issue of undocumented citizenship has commanded the attention of human rights advocates and development practitioners for a considerable time now. Articles 7 and 8 of the 1989 United Nations (UN) Convention on the Rights of the Child declare that national governments should register children immediately after birth and that children should enjoy, from birth, the right to acquire and maintain a nationality.[7] The current campaign by The UN Refugee Agency (UNHCR) to end statelessness, marked by the slogan "I Belong," advocates that "No states have populations which are entitled to nationality under law but which cannot acquire documentary proof of nationality." The campaign specifically includes undocumented nationals owing to an awareness of the fact that they often end up functionally stateless. In this light, development practitioners from organizations such as the UN Children's Fund (UNICEF), Plan International, World Vision, the Open Society Foundation, and Namati have been actively engaged in finding ways to enhance documentation among marginalized individuals and communities for the sake of their social, economic, and political empowerment.

Interestingly, however, academic political scientists have paid relatively little attention to the matter of undocumented nationals.[8] There has instead been much scrutiny of situations in which people lack IDs because they lack state membership altogether (e.g. highly persecuted minorities, people who have fallen victim to border changes and state successions, and various nomadic groups) and of situations involving immigrants who may be citizens elsewhere but not in their country of long-term residence (e.g. people of Mexican or Central American origin with irregular status in the United States and guest workers in some European countries, before recent changes). Political scientists' neglect of birth registration among those with a legal entitlement to nationality is especially puzzling given that it is the beginning of an individual's relationship to the state and the precondition for broader citizenship rights, including the eligibility to vote. On the birth certificate in particular, one researcher writes, "For a document as important as the birth certificate there has been surprisingly little discussion of its nature, contents, and significance" (Clapton 2014: 209). Nationals without documents have received even less coverage in the media, although perhaps this is no wonder considering that "For the most part, evidentiary challenges to citizenship occur in dark corners of bureaucracies, their details only vaguely articulable even by those directly affected" (Stevens 2017: 16). Instead, journalists are more inclined to feature stories in which the denial of state membership involves visible frontal conflict, resulting in vulnerable populations being detained or forcibly driven out of countries that do not want them. Occasionally, however, stories surface about

---

[7] See Simmons (2009: 312–317) on the Convention on the Rights of the Child.

[8] Notable exceptions include Scott (1998), Blitz (2009), Blitz and Lynch (2012), Hunter and Brill (2016), and Lawrance and Stevens (2017). Breckenridge and Szreter (2012) outline the political history of a wide-range of identity-registration systems. Political scientist Joseph Wong, founder of the Reach Project, has also underscored the importance of birth registration for social provisioning. See Wong (2015) and Wong *et al.* (2016).

"citizens without proof" (Brennan Center for Justice 2006), even in developed countries such as the United States.[9] Their resulting inability to receive basic social assistance and to vote has put their plight into the spotlight.[10] Of those currently without a birth certificate in the United States, most are older African-Americans who were born at home in rural areas of the South. Their marginalization is shared by a subset of older Native Americans.[11] Less common, but noteworthy, are contemporary cases of US children whose parents sought an "off-the-grid" existence and never registered their births. Such children tend to be born at home, schooled at home, and not vaccinated.[12] A common theme that runs across these different examples is the difficulty that the undocumented person encounters when trying to obtain delayed registration and certification.

The purpose of this Cambridge Element is to draw attention to the important yet understudied issue of "undocumented citizenship," that is, of nationals who lack the official papers necessary to be recognized as full citizens in their countries. It focuses on understanding the gray zone between full-on statelessness and officially validated citizenship.[13] With special reference to the foundational issue of birth registration and certification, *Undocumented Nationals* describes the scope of the problem, where it is concentrated geographically, and the kinds of people that are most afflicted by it. It also identifies, analyzes, and illustrates the causes, consequences, and remedies associated with two different causal patterns of undocumented citizenship or evidentiary statelessness,[14] terms that will be used interchangeably with undocumented nationality. In one pattern, a dearth in documentation is more the consequence of governmental neglect, omission, or failure than of intentional deprivation. In the other pattern, it is the result of deliberate discrimination, generally against racial or ethnic minority groups. Improvements in birth registration rest on a combination of factors that stimulate enhanced societal demand, together with increased state supply or facilitation of documentation. The likelihood of increasing birth registration depends largely on the initial causes of

---

[9] See Bradley (2017). See also Kurth and Roelofs (2017).

[10] See National Public Radio (2018).

[11] See Granillo (2014).

[12] Tara Westover's 2018 best-selling memoir, *Educated*, recounts her experiences of this kind. Raised in a Mormon survivalist family in rural Idaho, Westover spent her early years isolated from schools, medical facilities, and the state's civil registry. Her later experience in trying to obtain delayed registration in order to make her way into mainstream society proved to be no easy task. See also Radiolab (2016).

[13] Following common usage in contemporary international law, I use the terms "citizen" and "national" interchangeably in reference to the legal relationship between an individual and a state, whereby the state recognizes and guarantees the rights of the individual. I make similar reference to people with "state membership."

[14] This term should be credited to Jacqueline Stevens (2017).

underregistration, the strength of individual and state incentives for closing the gap, and the appropriateness of bureaucratic measures adopted to do so. The hopeful news is that developing-country governments that are seriously committed to change, even those that are nontotalitarian in nature, can make significant progress in this area. For example, Morocco, Cambodia, Cape Verde, Djibouti, and Honduras all have a gross national income (at purchasing power parity) of less than US$5,000 per capita but nonetheless have birth-registration rates around 90 percent. Ample political will, together with well-targeted resources around a handful of well-chosen policy measures, have resulted in considerable gains being made, even in low-income countries with limited overall state capacity. International organizations and non-governmental organizations (NGOs) can play a useful role when developing-country governments seek out their contributions in terms of expertise and resources.

Undocumented Nationals is organized as follows. Section 2 presents a conceptual and descriptive overview of undocumented nationality. In the broader context of clarifying what the phenomenon is and is not, it provides information on the number, kind, and location of people who suffer from undocumented nationality, specifically with reference to the lack of the foundational document of a birth certificate. The section makes an important first-cut broad distinction between the *legal* denial of nationality status, which results in entirely stateless individuals, and the *administrative* denial of nationality status, which leads to undocumented nationals. It then distinguishes between two variants of undocumented nationals: those who lack documents owing to acts of state omission and those who lack documents owing to state commission. In the former instance, the state's inattention to stimulating demand for and facilitating documentation can have the de facto effect of leaving poor and marginalized people without official papers. In the latter variant, government officials and street-level bureaucrats deliberately withhold essential documentation from those they wish to exclude as full members of the national club. Interestingly, both of the two scenarios put people in a situation that is the opposite of what Kamal Sadiq (2008) calls "paper citizens" or "documentary citizens," whereby paperwork, often acquired illegally, confers citizenship on immigrants with no legal basis for it.

Section 3 focuses on the first variant of undocumented citizenship, in which low levels of birth registration reflect state neglect and failure more than an intentional effort to exclude specific groups of people.[15] The argument it develops and illustrates is the following: if the state's previous civil registration

---

[15] This is not to say that there is not occasional discrimination exercised on the part of individual registrars.

system was not sufficiently affordable and "user-friendly" to incorporate all nationals, governments need to take active measures to both stimulate societal demand for registration and facilitate the state's provisioning of it. In other words, it is unrealistic to think that previous incentives and procedures for civil registration, gone unmodified, will attract new registrants. Improving birth registration demands a change in strategy. Beyond diminishing the economic costs of registering a child, the challenge of getting unregistered populations to enter the civil registry involves finding ways to reach groups that typically have limited engagement with public institutions (Dunning *et al.* 2014: 6). Facilitating their access to registration demands active state outreach and sometimes requires flexibility with respect to languages and cultural practices other than those dominant in the country.

The cases used to illustrate these dynamics are all from Latin America, although many of them apply well beyond the region. Many people assume that claiming nationality is generally not a problem in the Americas owing to the widespread prevalence of the *jus soli* principle (automatic citizenship based on birth in the territory of a state), which does give children a natural advantage over those born in Europe, Africa, and the Middle East (Vengoechea Barrios 2017: 25).[16] However, for *jus soli* norms to protect people from situations of effective or de facto statelessness, they must be accompanied by full birth registration, a situation that has not existed historically and that remains elusive in some countries of the region. Despite being the developing world region with the lowest percentage of unregistered births (UNICEF 2016a: 6), there are still three million children under the age of five who are unregistered in Latin America and the Caribbean.

After exploring the historical and contemporary factors that account for underregistration in Latin America, Section 3 analyzes the conditions under which birth-registration rates have improved. The quest for social inclusion stands out as a central motive of the state for increasing coverage in recent years. Countries ranging in economic strength and state capacity levels, from Bolivia to Brazil, have made improvements stemming from this pursuit. Another motive, one that can coexist with enhancing social inclusion, is the desire to keep track of populations that were dislocated owing to armed conflicts. Peru and Colombia are examples of countries that reflect both incentives

---

[16] Some thirty-plus countries, most of them located in the Americas, grant citizenship automatically based on the birth-right principle (Gelb & Metz 2018: 51). A partial exception in some Latin American countries concerns children born of parents who are working abroad in the service of another country (e.g. foreign diplomats and military personnel). In addition, the Dominican Republic has tried to narrow the scope of birth right citizenship, as discussed in Section 3.

simultaneously. To increase the registration and certification of births, governments in these countries and elsewhere in the region have implemented a variety of measures to lift the economic and logistical burdens on families of low-income and education levels, especially those who live in remote rural areas and who may not speak Spanish or Portuguese.

Section 4 focuses on the second variant of undocumented citizenship, whereby not having a registered birth is the consequence of explicit discrimination against groups of people owing to their ascriptive attributes. This variant is intensely political and generally arises in countries where *jus sanguinis* norms prevail, that is, where nationality is determined by what is judged to be the nationality of the parents at the time of a child's birth (Vengoechea Barrios 2017: 18). Contexts that allow bureaucrats to decide whether or not applicants' ancestors were "true" nationals leave far more room for discrimination than those where the guiding principle of citizenship is the state that pertains to the territory of one's birth. As the section shows, in several notable instances, governments have shied away from barring applicants' state membership as a matter of official (legal) policy and instead have erected unreasonable barriers to applicants' ability to access nationality-granting documents. In short, by deliberately depriving nationals of documents, governments can effectively impede them from becoming full citizens. Because it is the state's exclusive prerogative to recognize the facts of a person's birth as entitling them to membership or not, and because no other entity but the state can provide official documentation, attaining full citizenship in cases of deliberate discrimination in *jus sanguinis* systems can be challenging indeed.

The two cases analyzed in Section 4 illustrate somewhat different versions of this dynamic. A clear-cut case of depriving people from a specific ethnic group of official papers in order to block them from attaining full citizenship involves the Nubians of Kenya, who have long struggled to obtain the documentation that would allow them to successfully realize the Kenyan nationality to which they are legally entitled. In another example, the Dominican Republic's recent efforts to diminish or even eliminate the citizenship of Dominicans of Haitian descent is also ostensibly documents based. Many such individuals were born in the Dominican Republic under a permissive *jus soli* framework but were never registered, much less certified. Their Dominican-born parents and grandparents went generally unregistered as well. Following the government's initiative in 2010 to retroactively shift the basis of Dominican nationality to align with a *jus sanguinis* framework, such individuals have been hard pressed to (re)claim Dominican citizenship given the requirement that they provide birth documents that they do not have. In both instances, central to the state's efforts to exclude "outsiders" from becoming fully fledged members of the national club is the deprivation of nationality-realizing documents, together with demands that individuals present official papers (knowing full well they are unlikely to have them).

Section 5 concludes the Element. The conclusion in Section 5 begins by briefly revisiting the themes and examples presented in the previous sections. In particular, the fact that even countries of relatively low-income levels and state capacity can make progress in this area, should they wish to do so, is highlighted. Undertaking the right set of policy interventions and enlisting the assistance of international organizations are key in this regard. Admittedly, countries that are travelling the last mile to include all citizens, as opposed to countries that are starting from a much lower point, face somewhat different situations. The conclusion will reiterate the role of politics in affecting the recognition and provisioning of nationality-granting documents, as well as draw attention to the crucial role of policy reforms in facilitating or obstructing the documentation process. Political will, accompanied by a set of well-chosen and effectively implemented policies, can greatly improve birth-registration coverage, even in countries with low overall state capacity and modest resources. A lack of political will, not to mention active resistance on the part of the state and its bureaucrats, generally results in undocumented nationals having to overcome excessively high hurdles. Recent patterns of inclusion and exclusion in a country's civil registry reflect these contrasting dynamics.

2 Evidentiary Statelessness in Perspective

This section presents a conceptual and a descriptive overview of undocumented nationality, also referred to as evidentiary statelessness. The first part explains who these unregistered children and adults tend to be and where they live. The second part places the phenomenon of undocumented nationality in the broader context of discussions about statelessness. It defines various categories of the reasons why people lack documents. A contrast is drawn between legal and administrative sources of statelessness. For example, some people lack nationality-granting documents because they belong to no state, legally. Others have a plausible legal claim to state membership but lack the documents to prove it. In other words, they suffer from what are mainly administrative deficiencies. Some may be in this situation because of documentary challenges that arise from state neglect and failure. Others find themselves in this situation owing to active discrimination against given individuals and groups. These situations are further developed and illustrated in Sections 3 and 4.

Descriptive Overview: Who and Where are the Unregistered?

Regions of the world vary considerably in terms of how many people go unregistered at birth. As the bar graph in Figure 1a shows, Eastern and Southern Africa has the lowest average registration coverage (41 percent). Sub-Saharan Africa is the next lowest (43 percent). West and Central Asia is somewhat higher (45 percent), followed by South Asia (60 percent). Latin America and the Caribbean (95 percent) and the Middle East and North Africa (92 percent) have considerably higher rates, but fall short of universal registration. Given the low standard for a birth being counted as registered (i.e. generally, a caretaker reporting that they have registered the birth, even if there is no accompanying birth certificate), the real rates of registration are in all likelihood lower.[17] Moreover, nearly everywhere where registration is low, even those who are registered frequently lack the certificate that confirms their registered birth. Especially for people born before digital registries came into existence (most people), the actual certificate is of practical importance for proving age and nationality. For example, at an immunization clinic, the health practitioner, who lacks access to the civil registry, will ask to see a birth certificate. In all regions, averages mask significant cross-country variation, as the choropleth map in Figure 1b reveals. Furthermore, country averages mask significant internal variation in registration, as discussed later on.

Whether a child is born in a rural or an urban setting constitutes one of the most important predictors of birth registration status in every developing region, as the bar graph in Figure 1a shows.[18] The disadvantage of being born in a rural setting, along with the other disadvantages discussed below, applies far more in countries with overall lower registration rates. Whereas the reported world average for registration of under-fives is 59 percent in rural areas, it rises to 82 percent in urban areas. The reasons for this gap include the fact that parents in rural areas are generally less likely to see a benefit to registering their children and are therefore less likely to take active steps to do so. Also crucial is the higher proportion of babies born at home in rural settings than in urban areas. The first step toward civil registration is the official reporting of a live birth, which institutions such as clinics and hospitals generally carry out with greater ease than the midwives who oversee home births. Furthermore, civil registries

---

[17] The methodological challenges of counting people who are not registered are daunting. Especially in settings where it is difficult to determine how many live births took place in a given year (e.g. where there is a high percentage of out-of-hospital births), it is difficult to know with certainty how many people went unregistered. See Harbitz and Tamargo (2009: 3–4) on how researchers arrive at these estimates.

[18] See also a well-done quantitative evaluation of this fact for birth certificate coverage in ninety-four countries (Bhatia *et al.* 2017).

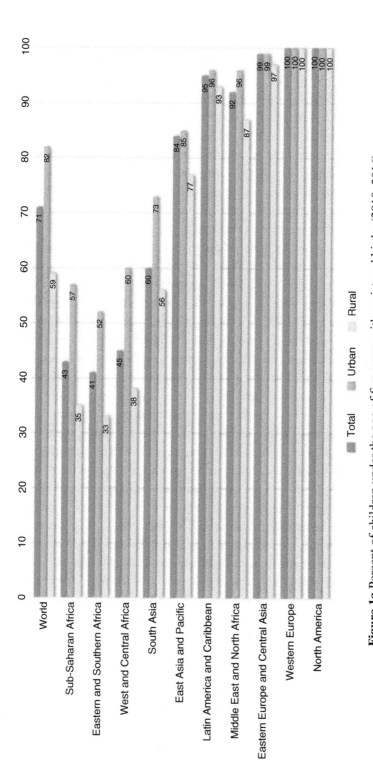

Figure 1a Percent of children under the age of five years with registered births (2010–2016)

Note: The data refers to the most recent year available during the period specified. The data includes children whose caretaker reported that they had a registered birth, even when this statement was unaccompanied by proof in the form of a birth certificate. The data excludes China.

Source: https://data.unicef.org/topic/child-protection/birth-registration/

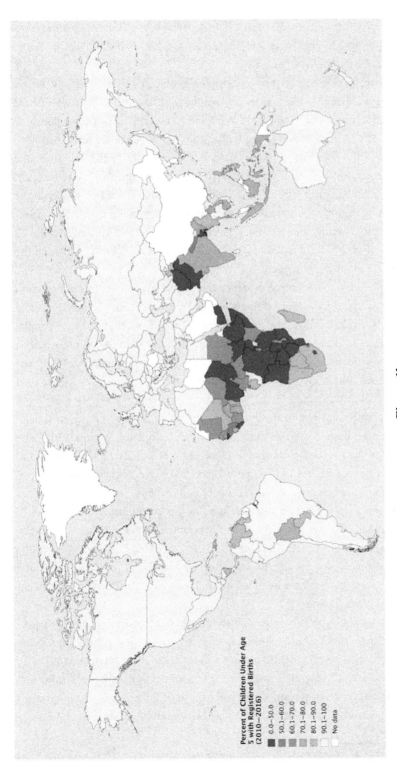

Percent of Children Under Age 5 with Registered Births (2010–2016)

- 0.0–50.0
- 50.1–60.0
- 60.1–70.0
- 70.1–80.0
- 80.1–90.0
- 90.1–100
- No data

Figure 1b

are typically farther away for people living in rural areas. Beyond the direct cost of registering and certifying a child, travel to a civil registry from a remote region can be prohibitively costly.

Coming from a poor family constitutes another consistent disadvantage, one that is especially marked in the regions (and countries) with the lowest registration rates. For example, in West and Central Africa, whereas only 27 percent of children under five years of age are registered in the lowest-income quintile, 70 percent of children under five years are registered from the wealthiest quintile. The role of family income in registration is marked, even in many Latin American and Caribbean countries, which make up the developing region with the highest registration rates in the world. For example, in the Dominican Republic, in the lowest-income quintile, only 73 percent of children (under five years) have a registered birth, while, in the wealthiest quintile, 98 percent do.[19]

In addition, there is ample evidence that being indigenous or coming from an ethnic minority group diminishes one's chances of being registered (UNHCR 2017a). There are several reasons for this. Among older people, some are unregistered and lack documents because colonial administrations did not consider registration to be a right of indigenous populations (HelpAge International 2011: 2). The wariness that many minority groups harbor toward the state for historical reasons often causes them to continue shying away from civil registries and public institutions in the contemporary era, even though there is no official barrier to their registration. Indigenous groups and ethnic minorities also tend to live in the more remote regions of their countries, precluding ready access to registration services. Not commanding the official language of the country and having names and perhaps even naming practices that do not align with mainstream cultural norms constitute further sources of isolation and effective exclusion. Naming practices in some cultures extend to not assigning formal names to babies until they are older. Finally, if present-day governments do not provide much in the way of social protection to ethnic minorities, people who are inhibited by such factors have little concrete incentive to overcome them.

Coming from a country where existing legal, administrative, and even cultural practices make it difficult for mothers to carry out the registration process on their own also works against registration coverage (Plan International 2012). There are several separate issues here. The most extreme involves rules that see nationality being passed exclusively through fathers, which complicates registration if the father lacks or loses his own proof of nationality or becomes

---

[19]   https://data.unicef.org/topic/child-protection/birth-registration/

separated from his children. This can potentially result in full-on stateless-ness. Less extreme but common are rules that bar mothers from carrying out the logistics of registering their children. Yet another factor involves the stigmatizing obstacles that mothers can encounter when registering a child out of wedlock (even if they can legally do so). Practices such as Latin American registrars writing "illegitimate child" in place of a father's name, or making a registered child take the mother's last name twice to fulfill the Spanish tradition of having two last names, are significant deterrents. Similarly, in Indonesia, having only the mother's name inscribed on the birth certificate if a child is born outside a legally registered marriage (which is frequently the case among the poor owing to the sheer cost of registering a marriage) is also stigmatizing, given the perceived implication of illegitimacy. Not surprisingly, even if their parents are religiously married, children born of nonregistered legal marriages are considerably less likely to have birth certificates than those born to parents whose marriages have been registered (Gelb 2015, Sumner 2015a, b).

Finally, since timeliness in registration is crucial, any factors that are likely to delay registration can have a compounding negative effect over time on the likelihood of a birth being registered and may result in no registration occurring at all. Beyond all the factors discussed above, situa-tions of dislocation such as migration and armed conflict frequently impede timely registration.[20] Proving that a birth took place where and when it did, associating the given child with its parents, and finding witnesses to attest to key facts if necessary all become more difficult with the passage of time. Adolescents or adults who try to secure documentary evidence of their birth-place and parentage for the first time often find it exceedingly costly and difficult to do so. Even if they succeed, they may well have missed out on important opportunities in the interim.

Notably, there is one frequent demographic disadvantage that does not apply very widely when it comes to birth registration: the sex of the child. Female children do not tend to show a higher rate of nonregistration than male children. In contrast to the large differences in education and health care between girls

---

[20] As a contemporary case in point, the UNHCR (2014) estimates that over 75 percent of the babies born to Syrian refugees since their arrival in Lebanon have gone unregistered amidst the current conflict. Since Syrian nationality is transmitted paternally, if a child's father is Syrian, they are entitled to Syrian nationality. Yet, given that many fathers are absent, dead, or simply lack the means to prove their state membership, many children will languish for years without civil birth registration and will probably face serious problems claiming their nationality later in life. Situations such as these are why child-protection advocates emphasize the need to set up birth-registration procedures in conflict environments (UNICEF Innocenti Research Centre 2007).

and boys in many countries, there are only eight countries where a significant gap exists in the birth-registration coverage between girls and boys (Bhatia *et al.* 2017: 7). It is the case, however, that documents that pertain to people later in life, such as formal work cards and national IDs, are more likely to be acquired by men (Buvinic & Carey 2019). Greater interaction with the public sphere – for example, in military service and employment – induces men to seek out these documents more than women do. Nonetheless, women are at a disadvantage without these papers, reinforcing their inferior position and vulnerability.

Conceptual Overview

Figure 2 is intended to shed light on the various reasons why people lack nationality status and the corresponding documents. It emphasizes the state's position (the supply side or provisioning of documents) more than people's interest in becoming documented (the demand side), which will be recognized and systematically integrated into the analyses in Sections 3 and 4. All four categories lead to a lack of nationality-granting documents. The basic division between the categories is between people who lack official papers because they lack legal entitlement to nationality in the territory where they reside and people who in principle have state membership but cannot prove it. The most extreme situation of the former group corresponds to the far-right category in Figure 2, namely when people belong to no state at all and hence lack valid nationality-granting documents. These are the truly stateless of the world. A less extreme instance of the legal denial of nationality status concerns people who are nationals somewhere but lack state membership in the country where they have long resided and hope to keep residing. Lacking citizenship or even legal residence, they are undocumented immigrants or immigrants with irregular status. By contrast, the two categories on the left in Figure 2 refer to people who have a legal claim to nationality but lack the documents to prove it, for reasons that are more administrative in nature. The distinction between having a claim to nationality and having the documents

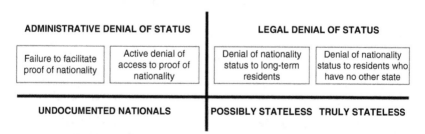

Figure 2 Reasons why people lack nationality-granting documents

to substantiate that claim is a meaningful one. People who fall into the left two categories in Figure 2 suffer from a combination of being uninformed, deterred, and/or denied when it comes to obtaining nationality-granting documents. Those are the people that this Element seeks to put into stark relief. The empirical cases in Sections 3 and 4 deal exclusively with the left-hand side of the diagram.

The remainder of this section is dedicated to examining/illustrating each category and its implications for possessing or acquiring official documents. It briefly outlines what undocumented nationals are not, before proceeding to discuss what they are.

People Who Lack State Membership Anywhere

This situation describes the much-covered plight of the truly stateless, of which there are now estimated to be between ten and fifteen million in the world. People in this category of legal statelessness lack official papers because they belong to no state. In other words, the source of their deprivation is more fundamental than simply lacking documents. Those in this situation tend to belong to highly persecuted minority groups (e.g. the Rohingya of Myanmar or the Kurds in various countries), are victims of decolonization or state dissolution and succession and find themselves without legal standing in a new country (e.g. after the break-up of the Soviet Union and Yugoslavia[21]), or are caught between conflicting nationality laws owing to their mother and father having different nationalities.[22] Marked in some parts of sub-Saharan Africa, there is also the plight of orphans of unknown origin in countries where citizenship is based on parentage. The HIV/AIDS epidemic has worsened this problem. There have also been several notorious historic instances where people who previously had been fully fledged citizens were arbitrarily deprived of their

---

[21] Large numbers of Roma got caught in the dissolution of the Socialist Federal Republic of Yugoslavia in the early 1990s. The Law on Citizenship of the former Yugoslav Republic of Macedonia, enacted in 1992, provided that citizens of the predecessor republic could become citizens of the newly created state (Macedonia) if they legally resided in the territory of the former Yugoslav Republic of Macedonia at the time of the dissolution and if they applied for naturalization within one year. Many Roma missed this window of opportunity, in part because they did not realize that they were not citizens of the country in which they continued to live. Others were unaware of the deadline or the steps that needed to be taken. As a result, "many became foreigners in the country in which they were born and had spent most of their lives" (UNHCR 2017b: 22–23). Children of this group probably became victims of their parents' statelessness as well. For more information on the Roma, see Barany (2002), Organization for Security and Co-operation in Europe (2005), Fleck and Rughinis (2008), Rozzi (2011), de Verneuil (2016), Bhabha (2017), and European Roma Rights Centre (2017).

[22] In addition, at present, twenty-seven countries deny women the right to pass their nationality on to their children (UNHCR 2014). Action 3 of the UNHCR's Global Action Plan to End Statelessness urges these states to remove gender discrimination from nationality laws.

nationality through a change in laws or deliberate targeting (e.g. Jews who had been long-term citizens of Germany having their nationality revoked between 1933 and 1945). The Denaturalization Law of 1933, which remained in place until 1945, deprived not only German Jews but also other so-called "undesirables" of their previously held nationality. In a more recent example, in 1993, over three million former migrants from West Africa who had been considered nationals of Côte d'Ivoire had their citizenship revoked, ultimately leading to a civil war.[23] This lasted until 2011, when President Alassane Ouattara eliminated the exclusionary policies that were based on the concept of "Ivoirité," paving the way for hundreds of thousands of individuals to restore or obtain Ivorian nationality (Bah 2017). In all of the above situations, not possessing official documents reflects a deeper problem: the lack of state membership. The resolution of this requires fundamental legal changes.[24]

People without Nationality Status Where They Reside

Much attention has also been paid to situations in which people live for long periods of time in a country without attaining nationality and the associated documents.[25] Some of these situations put people at risk of statelessness. Others do not. For example, if children are brought to a given country illegally from another where neither they nor their parents are citizens, they may be stateless. If they are nationals of another country, however, they are not stateless, even if they have never spent much time in their country of legal nationality and do not speak the language of that country. A high-profile contemporary example of this latter situation involves the DREAMers, the unauthorized immigrants brought to the United States as children by their parents. The vast majority of these young people are not stateless because they were born in countries of birthright

---

[23] The Ivory Coast's total population when it gained independence (1960) was 3.7 million people, of which 13 percent were originally from outside the country. The subsequent basis of their exclusion rested on the charge that they had been born outside the new national borders. Most had immigrated to and settled in the country prior to independence (Adjami 2016: 8).

[24] Other examples of total legal statelessness include the following: a group of Syrian Kurds (now numbering about 160,000) who were negatively affected by a special census ordered by degree in 1962, as well as the Bidun in Kuwait, the Biharis in Bangladesh, and the Karana minority in Madagascar. In addition, in Lebanon, Syria, and the Gulf States, the descendants of those who were not included in the population registries created when the countries gained independence remain stateless today. In Thailand, it is estimated that there are over 400,000 people who are legally stateless. Many of the stateless in Thailand belong to hill tribes living in remote areas. They include members of the Akna, Hmong, Karen, Lanu, Lisu, and Shan ethnic communities. Some of the stateless fled into Thailand owing to conflicts in neighboring countries (including some Rohingya under the Burmese military regime) and never even received legal protection through refugee status.

[25] This differs from legal residency, which is always easier to obtain than citizenship and generally entitles a person to a variety of rights.

citizenship in the Americas. They became known as DREAMers after the introduction of the Development, Relief, and Education for Alien Minors (DREAM) Act. This legislation was first introduced in 2001 and was intended to (but still has not) put those who arrived as children on a path to citizenship. Many DREAMers report that they did not even know that they lacked legal standing in the United States until they were teenagers and could not get a driver's license. Rectifying their irregular status depends on the implementation of legal reforms, which have now been stalled in Congress for roughly a decade and a half.[26] Former guest workers in Europe (e.g. Turkish immigrants in Germany) constitute another example of the legal denial of citizenship. Although having state membership in Turkey, these immigrants had long resided in Germany. These so called "denizens" (Hammar 1985, 1990) had always enjoyed more interim legal standing than the DREAMers, including access to social protection, but nonetheless eventually sought to regularize their status completely. After three generations, they gained full legal standing as German nationals with the voting rights and documentation associated with their naturalizing country.

People Denied Access to Proof of Nationality

Crossing the central divide in Figure 2 from statelessness into the zone of "evidentiary statelessness" or "undocumented nationality" means going from predominantly legal to mainly administrative sources of exclusion. In general, people on the left-hand side (see Figure 2) of that divide (undocumented nationals) are better off than their counterparts with no nationality at all (or nationality in countries other than where they reside). However, undocumented nationals are not as protected as those with nationality and the corresponding documents. If proof of citizenship is the core problem of undocumented nationals, the solution rests on finding evidence of nationality. Yet, as stated powerfully by Bronwen Manby:

> The rules for proof of the facts on the basis of which nationality is claimed and for issuing documents that show that a person is recognized as a national are, in practice, often as important as the provisions of the law on the conditions that must be established. If there are onerous requirements or costs attached to proof of entitlement to nationality, then the fact that a person actually fulfils the conditions laid down in law may be irrelevant (Manby 2017: 116).

---

[26] Undocumented immigrants who also lack nationality-granting documents (beginning with birth registration) in their country of origin are highly vulnerable. This situation no doubt describes a fair number of those whose originating country is Mexico (Notimex 2015).

Overcoming such hurdles is especially difficult when state officials, with the intent to exclude, resort to the selective application of administrative red tape.

The ability of officials to engage in such discretion tends to be greater where *jus sanguinis* is the basis of state membership. For example, ethnic minorities in various sub-Saharan African countries often face difficulties in showing that they are legally entitled to state membership. The enduring practice of registrars not recording babies whose parents have no official identity (a common condition in a region of low birth registration and low national ID rates) makes being undocumented almost a hereditary condition. That registrars frequently demand hard-to-come-by proof that people's ancestors were in the country by a given time (a common proxy for membership by "blood") can lock people out of gaining the IDs that are essential to becoming full nationals.[27] In the absence of such proof, the charge is that the document seeker is not a "real" Kenyan or Ivorian, etc. Even if the requirements raised by state officials are based on shaky legal grounds, the rules are byzantine to the uneducated, who all too often are deterred and worn down by the application process. Needless to say, the extraction of bribes from vulnerable people also occurs with alarming regularity. It takes a committed state to overcome such practices on a systematic basis. Notably, however, the fact that some individuals – through sheer will of their own and/or good counsel (including activism by legal NGOs and their paralegal teams) – have been able to successfully overcome bureaucratic hurdles and obtain documentation suggests that nationality laws themselves are not always the core problem (Maru & Gauri 2018).

Interestingly, governments sometimes seem to choose between two strategies: on the one hand emphasizing that "the other" do not legally belong because they come from elsewhere and on the other hand (implicitly) recognizing that they have a claim to nationality but making it virtually impossible for them to realize it. The former route, which generates legal statelessness, can incur negative international opinion and even be in violation of international law. The latter, generally less controversial than the former, results in evidentiary statelessness. As discussed in Section 4, the shift that the government of the Dominican Republic made from denationalizing Haitian descendants altogether (between 2004 and 2014) to allowing them to seek Dominican nationality but with excessively high evidentiary criteria (2014 until now) demonstrates this dynamic. Kenya's treatment of the Nubians exemplifies a similar situation. Kenya's Nubian population was forcibly recruited from Sudan

---

[27] Sometimes, even those who have a record and a certificate of their birth experience problems in obtaining national IDs and passports, which are stronger indications of citizenship.

by the British army at the turn of the twentieth century. Like other groups in parts of Central and East Africa, their association with the colonial authorities put them at odds with postindependence governments (Blitz 2009: 10). The fact that they are Muslim has put them at further risk of being discriminated against, given the security frame that Kenyan officials now employ. In principle, Nubians had the right to Kenyan nationality when the new independent state was formed in 1963 and yet the group has battled evidentiary statelessness ever since. In 2010, it was (conservatively) estimated that at least 13 percent of Nubian adults were undocumented (Open Society Justice Initiative 2011a). Kenya does not deny this group Kenyan nationality through explicit laws. What it does do, however, is allow vetting committees the right to exercise wide discretion. A frequent line of questioning involves asking to see the documents of the person's parents and grandparents, which most people have great difficulty producing because of historical inequities in documentation. In short, many Nubians find themselves trapped in long-standing patterns of underdocumentation.

With respect to the Roma, there is an evidentiary counterpart to those who are legally stateless in places like Macedonia. The vast majority of Roma in the Western Balkans could potentially achieve documented nationality, but they run up against extraordinarily complicated administrative procedures, excessively high costs, and discriminatory treatment.[28] According to one source, "Bad administrative practices often enable discrimination and prejudice to be determinative of whether or not a person will be recognised as a citizen, particularly where officials have discretion in decision making" (European Roma Rights Centre 2017: 12). Discrimination creates a vicious cycle. Fear of the police owing to being undocumented inhibits such individuals from taking the step that obviously needs to be taken.[29]

People in Countries that Have Failed to Facilitate Proof of Nationality

Whereas the evidentiary problem described immediately above results from active discrimination, the state's failure to facilitate essential documentation can also be passive or through indirect discrimination. In other words, rules applied universally (e.g. sizable registration fees and onerous procedures) do not affect everyone equally. Because some individuals and groups cannot meet such requirements as well as others, they will effectively lag behind in

---

[28] The situation of the Roma in Western Europe is far from ideal but is arguably somewhat better than Eastern Europe as far as obtaining documents is concerned.

[29] In another "catch-22," there is a provision for free legal aid in Albania, but many Roma cannot provide sufficient documentation to be eligible for it (European Roma Rights Centre 2017: 13).

documentation coverage. The fuller inclusion of such groups thus rests on the development of policy interventions that take these disadvantages systematically into account and actively try to overcome them.

Examples of indirect discrimination abound. Many Latin American and Caribbean governments, for instance, have been negligent in registering vast numbers of marginalized people who have birthright citizenship. Patterns of underregistration reflect the legacy of inequality in the region. Whereas notables entered civil registries in the nineteenth century, followed in the twentieth century by middle-class professionals, urban workers, and eventually many poor people in urban shantytowns, those left out until recently (and sometimes even until now) are poor people who live in rural areas, especially if they are indigenous or Afro-descendants. The historic lack of concern for broad social inclusion meant that Latin American governments had little interest in making registration financially feasible and logistically accessible to all. High costs and complicated procedures exerted a disproportionate negative impact on marginalized populations (Plan International & UNICEF 2010). As Section 3 demonstrates, however, recent interest by Latin American and Caribbean governments in making their populations legible and furthering social inclusion stimulated a greater demand for documents and the introduction of policy measures that helped hundreds of thousands of people become documented within just a few years. In addition to awareness-raising campaigns, these initiatives included eliminating fees for timely and delayed registration, deputizing state agents to go on mobile registration drives, and encouraging registrars to install services in maternity clinics and to travel to schools where older, unregistered, children were seeking to enroll. More will be said about these and other facilitating procedures in the next section.

Turning to another area of the developing world, a major emerging country known for its poor record in registering the births of nationals is Indonesia. Indonesia's reported rate of nonregistration is 33 percent, although a major study recently conducted by the Australia Indonesia Partnership for Justice suspects that closer to 50 percent of all children may not have a birth certificate (Gelb 2015). Indonesian law requires parents to register a child's birth within the first sixty days, during which time registration is free as stipulated by the federal government. However, to register a birth, parents must present a number of documents, including a birth reference certificate from the place where the mother gave birth, a birth reference from the village office, the parents' marriage certificate, the parents' Indonesian identity card, and the parents' Indonesian family card (Arasindo & Partners 2012). Meeting these requirements is exceedingly difficult for many parents, especially for those who are poor and live in rural areas. Given that roughly half of all Indonesians live in rural villages (Plan International 2016), a large segment of the population is effectively excluded from civil registration. For many, the cost of obtaining these prior documents is prohibitive and the bureaucratic hurdles involved are simply too high to overcome. In effect, the system discriminates against those who cannot afford to travel to obtain documents or to pay off-the-record fees to the middlemen and registrars themselves that are necessary to secure such documents (Duff *et al.* 2016). Parents are charged extra if they have exceeded the sixty-day window for registering a birth. The physical distances that need to be travelled can be great, as any transactions involving the civil registry need to be conducted primarily at the district (as opposed to the village) level. Sometimes, people even need to travel to other islands to interact with registrars (UNICEF Indonesia 2014). This lack of accessibility is a common problem across the developing world.

Indonesia places a further barrier between children and the registration of their births: the requirement that their parents (Muslim and non-Muslim alike) present a legal marriage certificate. Considerable numbers of Indonesians who are wed in religious ceremonies do not understand that a religiously recognized marriage does not count as a legal marriage. Others do but nonetheless lack an official marriage certificate because of the prohibitive costs involved. With official marriage certificates costing as high as US$80 (Platt 2009), it is no wonder that approximately 76 percent of the poorest couples do not obtain them (Plan International 2016). Finally, although the Indonesian state now recognizes interfaith marriages, in the past it did not and, in practice, civil servants often still block mixed faith couples from civil registration. Children whose parents can present a formal marriage certificate can have both parents listed on the birth certificate, whereas children whose parents are not legally married (even if they are religiously married) have only their mothers listed (Sumner 2015a, b). In the latter case, there is no legally recognized relationship between the child and the father. Because of the stigma associated with births out of wedlock, parents are reluctant to register their child if the birth certificate cannot have both parents' names on it. It is estimated that 75 percent of children born to nonlegal unions are not registered for a birth certificate (Gelb 2015). Clearly, the road to improving birth-registration rates in Indonesia rests on shrinking the distances between the population and civil registrars, finding ways to diminish petty corruption by brokers who overcharge vulnerable individuals for documents, and relaxing the rules regarding official marriage certificates.

The United States, which is well known for its generous birthright citizenship, has its own "skeletons" that involve undocumented nationals. According to the Brennan Center for Justice, as many as 7 percent of US citizens, equivalent to 13 million people, cannot produce documentation to prove their citizenship (Brennan Center for Justice 2006). Although historians, demographers, and the public health community have long known about the under-registration of births in the United States,[30] the problem has only recently surfaced in the media in connection with electoral disenfranchisement. A not insignificant segment of the population that was born well into the 1950s was never registered. Being poor, nonwhite, and born at home in a rural area (especially in the South), as well as having an uneducated mother, were all risk factors for nonregistration (Shapiro 1950). According to one source, "Tens of thousands of babies were born off the grid" (Lubrano 2014). The bureaucratic difficulties they have faced as adults in obtaining delayed registration or replacing lost certificates have hindered their ability to lay claim to the benefits and rights of citizenship. Being unable to exercise the right to vote is only the tip of the iceberg. Without official identification, which generally begins with a birth certificate, it is exceedingly difficult to collect (age-dependent) social security benefits, sign up for disability payments, obtain subsidized housing, sign a lease, open a bank account, or secure a job.[31]

It is not just the elderly in the United States whose lives are complicated by lacking basic documentation. Teenagers who have left their broken homes, often even those in the foster care system, frequently find themselves without birth certificates.[32] The same is true for some exoffenders who, when leaving prison, need to either acquire vital forms of identification for the first time or recover them if they had them prior to incarceration (Pearce 2017). State data also show that many US citizen children lack the documentation required for their parents or guardians to apply for or renew their Medicaid coverage (Ross 2007). Although the requirement to show a birth certificate or passport as a form of ID was intended to diminish Medicaid applications among immigrants who falsely declared US citizenship, the requirement has inadvertently dropped

---

[30]   See Shapiro (1950), Rosenwaike and Hill (1996), Landrum (2015), and Pearson (2015). As late as 1940, sixteen US states had a birth-registration rate of less than 90 percent. When the United States became involved in World War II, millions of US residents needed to document their citizenship to work in the defense industry and were unable to do so because they lacked a US birth certificate. A combination of child labor laws, the Social Security Act of 1935, and the birth certificate crisis in World War II spurred documentation among many US residents. Nonetheless, a more marginalized segment of the population remained subject to nonregistration.

[31]   An author interview on November 26, 2018, with Gregory Markus, Executive Director of Detroit Action Commonwealth, revealed that, when the organization was founded, "help with obtaining ID documents" was the single most important item that people in area soup kitchens mentioned that they needed.

[32]   The radio program "Texas Standard" aired a four-part series in February and March 2019 that explored the plight of adolescents aging out of the Texas foster care system without vital documents to prove their US citizenship. See Diaz and Fogel (2019).

enrollments among otherwise eligible African-American and white children who are US citizens but do not have vital documents.[33]

The fact that birth registration in the United States is carried out by individual states – each with different rules – complicates efforts to authenticate one's existence years after the fact. Sometimes, it is even necessary to identify the county or municipality of one's birthplace to have a certificate created or replaced.[34] For those who were born decades ago and moved far away from their place of birth, applying for delayed registration and/or certification has generally proven to be quite difficult. In an effort to avoid fraud, the rules sometimes require applicants to prove that they were not registered under a different name, which is no easy task. In extreme instances (generally only possible with the help of legal aid), going back to census records can unlock the past. The well-known "catch-22" of documentation – that one needs to prove his or her identity to even get an ID – is painfully apparent, even in the United States, as encapsulated by the headline of one feature story about the problem: "I am somebody, I just can't prove it."[35]

Conclusion

This section's central purpose was to provide an overall framework for under-standing different forms and bases of statelessness. The main divide it sketched out was between the administrative and legal bases by which nationality is denied. This Element is devoted to understanding the link between the admin-istrative denial of nationality status and the resulting situations of evidentiary statelessness: one based on state neglect and failure and the other based on overt state discrimination. Regardless of which type a person suffers from, the distinction between being a national or citizen, in principle, and having the official papers to prove it is an important one in the modern world. Possessing official proof of nationality is crucial not only inside the borders of one's own country but also when one is abroad, especially in circumstances involving conflict and forced dislocation.

Birth registration is a joint function of parents' ability to perceive the benefits of a birth certificate for their children and the ease with which they can obtain it, which depends on how committed the state is to implementing procedures that are understandable, affordable, and accessible to all. Generally, this

---

[33] Interestingly, this effect has not occurred among US citizen children of Hispanic origin. It may well be the case that parents of such children take special care to secure their vital documents in case they are suspected of being in the United States illegally (Ross 2007).

[34] Some states make some provision for religious records to show parentage and birthdates, but many baptismal records do not include the vital fact of birthplace (Ross 2007).

[35] Bradley (2017) and Kurth and Roelofs (2017).

commitment stems from prior goals, which can include a pursuit of greater social inclusion, an effort to establish more social control, and the simple desire to have the data necessary to operate a more modern civil registration and vital statistics system in general, with all the individual and collective benefits that such a system entails.

Drawing on experiences from Latin America, the next section focuses on the variant of evidentiary statelessness that stems from de facto, more than intentional, discrimination. With reference to societal demand for and state interest in birth registration, it analyzes the political conditions under which progress has been made and the policies that have brought about this success. Lessons for other developing countries are pointed out along the way.

3 State Neglect and Unregistered/Uncertified Citizenship: Illustrations from Latin America

This section focuses on evidentiary statelessness that results from the state's historic failure to facilitate proof of nationality. It demonstrates that administrative neglect of this kind can result indirectly in discrimination against individuals and groups who lack the wherewithal to meet steep bureaucratic requirements. Such individuals may be deterred from even trying if they do not perceive that there are enough benefits from having a registered birth. Indeed, birth registration is a joint function of societal incentives, on the one hand, and state interests and capabilities, on the other. Change can occur fairly readily if states provide people with reasons to register and if they ease the process of registration through key administrative reforms, even in the face of overall gaps in state capacity.

This section draws on experiences from Latin America to analyze and illustrate the historic reasons for nonregistration among marginalized populations, as well as the factors that have led such populations to enter the civil registries of their countries in recent years. Politics and policy serve as critical explanatory factors. Inattention to birth registration historically went hand in hand with governments excluding the most challenged segments of the population from the benefits of emerging welfare states. The recent commitment to improving documentation on the part of many governments stemmed from formalizing social protection for a broader range of the population, and with this new focus came procedural reforms to lessen the administrative burdens associated with registering a child's birth. Although the specific cases presented in this section come from Latin America, many of the same dynamics apply in other developing regions.

The first part of this section identifies the people who have lacked birth registration in Latin America and analyzes the reasons behind this historic state of affairs, even in a region where proof of nationality (birth in the territory of a given state) is relatively straightforward. It examines society's uneven demand for documents and how difficult many governments made it to obtain them. The second part of this section examines the political impulse behind the increasing birth-registration coverage of recent years, which reshaped societal and state incentives alike. The third part of this section explains how the state has made registration more accessible and assesses the increase in registration rates that have resulted from these administrative interventions. Considerable progress has occurred even in low-income countries with low state capacity overall.

By way of background, the three basic documents required to establish a legal identity in most Latin American and Caribbean countries are a record of live birth, an actual birth certificate (which is provided only when a birth is recorded in the civil registry), and a national identity card. Without the first two documents, it is difficult to obtain the third (Harbitz & Tamargo 2009: 18). Of those who are undocumented, some people never had a registered or certified birth, others lost their original birth certificate and never recovered it (a situation that is made worse if the state's registration books are not in order), and some did register but their names were spelled erroneously, creating a mismatch with subsequent papers.

Who Was Undocumented and Why?

Which of the Latin American countries left large numbers of people out of their civil registries, especially until recently? Before answering this question, it pays to reiterate that data on this issue are patchy at best, given that unregistered children are generally invisible to the state.[36] The general consensus is that official figures overestimate the number of registered births owing to a reliance on parental reporting, among other problems.[37] It is also important to bear in mind that, despite notable improvements, roughly 1.3 million births annually are not registered in Latin America and the Caribbean and that approximately 6.5 million children aged five years and under do not have a birth certificate.

---

[36] Only when the number of live births is known with considerable certainty can demographers calculate the gap between that figure and the number who end up registering to arrive at an accurate estimate of nonregistration. A large number of deliveries outside institutional settings complicates the accuracy in determining the number of live births.

[37] For example, in 2011, the director of the Mexican civil registry estimated that at least 20 percent of the population lacked a birth certificate, a rate of nonregistration higher than most official figures (Valdés 2011). In addition, birth registration statistics vary significantly between sources in Colombia: the Colombia Demographic and Health Survey estimates that the underregistration of children is 9 percent, whereas the National Administrative Department of Statistics maintains that it is closer to 26 percent (UNICEF Innocenti Research Centre 2007: 15). Moreover, sources close to the ground in Paraguay, who prefer to remain anonymous, report higher rates of nonregistration than the official figures suggest.

Table 1 Percent of children under the age of five years with registered births

Countries	Averages	
	2000–2005	**2011–2016**
Argentina	91	100
Bolivia	74	87
Brazil	78.1	99
Chile	96	99
Colombia	84	96.8
Costa Rica	98	100
Dominican Republic	74.6	88
Ecuador	87	94
El Salvador	72	99
Guatemala	92.5	96
Haiti	69.7	80
Honduras	92.3	94
Jamaica	89	100
Mexico	78.8	95
Nicaragua	81.4	85
Paraguay	76	85
Peru	92.5	98
Uruguay	100	100
Venezuela	91.8	81

Note: The figures for 2000–2005 were compiled from a number of different sources. Contact the author for details. The data for 2011–2016 originate from https://data.unicef .org/topic/child-protection/birth-registration/

Table 1 shows the birth registration of those under five years for a range of Latin American countries in two periods. The initial period is about the first time for which (semi)reliable numbers exist across the region.[38]

As the table reveals, Latin American countries differ considerably in their birth-registration profiles. Whereas countries such as Brazil, Bolivia, the Dominican Republic, Ecuador, El Salvador, Guatemala, Haiti, Mexico, and Paraguay left large numbers of children out of their civil registries as late as 2000 (and far more in earlier decades), Argentina, Chile, Costa Rica, and Uruguay have long achieved near-universal registration.[39] Peru had low registration rates into the 1990s but lifted its numbers considerably before 2000.

---

[38] https://data.unicef.org/topic/child-protection/birth-registration/
[39] So has Cuba for *sui generis* reasons (i.e. being a communist country).

In general, countries with low historic rates of registration are home to large populations of poor people, a high proportion of rural residents, and large indigenous and/or Afro-descendant populations (Plan International & UNICEF 2010). These countries also tend to have weaker overall state capacity than their counterparts with higher birth-registration rates (Rice & Patrick 2008). Indeed, within the countries of lower overall registration, it is precisely the poor, those who live in rural areas, and those who are indigenous or Afro-descendants who are overrepresented among the unregistered. Being born at home, a well-known risk factor for underregistration, correlates positively with these demographic categories, as does having parents with low education levels, who may well be unregistered themselves. As a rule, the lower the rate of registration in a country, the more factors there are – such as family income, parental education, and place of residence – that create a divide between registered and unregistered citizens.[40]

Analyzing registration as a joint function of societal demand and state supply, we can understand why, in decades past, poor people in remote areas, especially those of indigenous origins and with low education levels, ended up with lower rates of registration. Put simply, from an immediate cost–benefit perspective, it was rational for such people to forego documentation. Not only was it expensive and logistically difficult to obtain documents, but there was also little purpose in doing so because such individuals received few state benefits and rights linked to possessing an official identity. Nor, for the most part, did Latin American states require citizens to become documented. Occupationally based provisioning of pensions and health care, coupled with most people's employment in the informal sector, rendered the poor ineligible for institutionalized social protection (Haggard & Kaufman 2008, Huber & Stephens 2012). For those excluded from formal assistance, social protection relied on personal relationships and handouts by local patrons, for which documents were unnecessary.

As regards indigenous people, because virtually no important ethnic parties existed and most political parties in the region did not go out of their way to court the votes of indigenous people, there was even less incentive for many to obtain an official identity (Madrid 2012). The demand for documents among indigenous populations was also suppressed by their wariness of public officials and institutions. Historic mistreatment of indigenous people by state authorities left a layer of culturally based resistance to registration among this population, given the potential that registration opened up for greater surveillance and control. No doubt many of these same considerations applied in the past, and

---

[40] UNICEF (2016a) is an excellent source that corroborates these points.

continue to apply today, to ethnic minority populations in other countries of the world. In short, the concrete benefits and rights conferred by a birth certificate were so implausible for many people that not pursuing registration and certification amounted to rational behavior, at least in the short term. No doubt many parents felt that they could register their children at a later date if need be, but generally this was easier said than done.

Considering the state and its provisioning of documents, several supply-side barriers made it even more understandable that marginalized populations did not register their babies. Obstacles to registration were high, some of which upper-income urban groups also faced, although with less of a negative impact on outcomes. Because entry into the civil registry usually entailed several direct and indirect economic costs, poverty was a risk factor for nonregistration. Parents had to go to registries (notary publics), present a record of live birth, and pay considerable fees, with there generally being two separate payments for registration and certification. Long distances between households and registries, which were typically greater in rural than in urban areas, compounded the logistical costs and hassles of registration. Living in a remote region also made it difficult to attain information about the procedural requirements of accessing public services (Corbacho & Rivas 2012). People's ignorance and confusion about such matters no doubt invited and reinforced rent-seeking behavior by registrars and other local officials, which governments did virtually nothing to diminish.

Being from an indigenous family exacerbated the impact of poverty and geographical remoteness. It continues to do so. In Guatemala, for example, although roughly 10 percent of the entire population lacks documents, approximately 40 percent of the indigenous population lacks documentation (Harbitz & Tamargo 2009: Table 2). As another illustration of this point, within Paraguay, only 70 percent of children who come from families that speak exclusively Guaraní at home are registered, which is 17 percentage points below those who speak both Guaraní and Spanish, and 24 percentage points below those who come from exclusively Spanish-speaking families (UNICEF 2016b: 80).

One reason for such figures is the greater likelihood of indigenous children being born at home and having no record of their births, which is an essential requirement for registration. Having such a record is virtually assured in a clinic or hospital.[41] Another reason relates to parents most likely lacking education

---

[41] The hospital's record is not the same as actual birth registration. In most Latin American countries, parents have needed to take the record of live birth to an official registrar for the birth to be put into the civil registry. In the case of hospital births, the hospital typically sends the record of live birth to the civil registry.

and documents themselves. In many countries, parents without official identification were barred from registering their children, effectively perpetuating intergenerational marginality (Harbitz & Tamargo 2009: 16, 30). Lacking fluency in Spanish (or Portuguese) also hindered parents' ability to navigate the bureaucracy and fill out the paperwork necessary to register a birth. Registrars in many countries were not familiar with indigenous languages; they dealt poorly (or not at all) with indigenous phonetics and either assumed or insisted on the presence of two surnames, as is the Spanish tradition. Thus, even when indigenous parents tried to register their children, the process sometimes resulted in incorrect and inconsistent spellings on documents. It even led to names that people never ended up adopting. In particular, if documents got lost and individuals did not remember how their names were recorded, the mismatch between individuals' various records created a bureaucratic nightmare. Finally, unresolved legal paternity was frequently the nail in the coffin. Throughout Latin America, mothers feared stigmatizing a child by officially declaring that he or she was fatherless (Ordóñez Bustamente & Bracamonte Bardález 2006: 85). Although this factor often also augured poorly for the registration of more affluent urban children, such children did not face other compounding hurdles.

In summary, for the better part of the twentieth century, many Latin American governments had little interest in pursuing a project of broad social and political inclusion. The region's civil registries reflected longstanding patterns of inclusion and exclusion. By the turn of the century (2000), gradual processes of modernization and a growth in public services had resulted in upwards of three-quarters of the population in this region having entered the civil registries, even in the most challenged countries. The majority of urban dwellers, even in low-income segments, were being registered, as documents were more demanded (even for children to start school) and civil registries had become more accessible. However, there was a stagnation or plateauing in these numbers that became evident over time. "Going the last mile" and reaching the most marginalized groups – those with limited contact with state institutions – would require a concerted effort. The strengthened commitment to social inclusion that many Latin American governments have embraced in the last twenty years has caused them to reach deeply into remote pockets of the national territory and enact reforms to bring the last segment of unregistered citizens into their countries' civil registries.

Why Latin American and Caribbean Governments Sought Broader Inclusion in Civil Registries

What, more precisely, motivated Latin American and Caribbean governments to close the remaining gaps in birth registration? In the second half of the 1990s, many recently democratized governments were under pressure to adopt a more inclusionary social policy agenda. The political momentum unleashed by democratization set politicians across the political spectrum in search of ways to address the poverty and inequality that had long plagued their countries. Beyond addressing gaps left by the previous welfare state model, governments felt compelled to respond to neoliberal economic reforms, which had reduced everything from food and utility subsidies to formal-sector employment (Huber & Stephens 2012: 175). A key goal was to create a minimum floor below which impoverished individuals and families would not fall. Income-transfer programs and noncontributory pensions spread in this context. Between 1997 and 2008, eighteen Latin American countries from across the political spectrum introduced national-level cash-transfer programs to provide income support for low-income families with children (Sugiyama 2011). Between 1990 and 2014, fourteen countries (also diverse in their ideological leanings) adopted a noncontributory pension scheme to prevent destitution among elderly people with no formal retirement income (Federación Internacional de Administradoras de Fondos de Pensiones 2011). The advent of these social-assistance policies created a surge in demand for birth certificates and other documents at the beginning of the twenty-first century.

Once social provisioning was bureaucratized, recipients would need to be formalized too. The new income transfers, which targeted benefits to individuals rather than to collectivities, could not be properly managed (i.e. run without fraud, corruption, or inefficiency) in the absence of legal IDs from all family members (Harbitz 2013).[42] Therefore, the problem was that the individuals most in need of such income transfers were precisely those that were least likely to have obtained documents at birth. To reach those who had fallen through the registration cracks in previous decades, Latin American governments would have to develop ways to facilitate documentation. Notably, some of the governments most committed to putting such policy reforms in place were in lower middle-income countries with low state capacity, such as Peru (in the 1990s) under the right-wing government of Alberto Fujimori, and Bolivia (more recently: 2006–present) under the left-wing president Evo Morales. In addition, although Brazil is neither a low-income country nor low in state capacity, it faced the challenge of reaching people located in isolated areas of a huge territory. A committed effort to enhance social inclusion

---

[42] This information is entered into unified registries, such as the Cadastro Único in Brazil, the Clave Única de Registro de Población in Mexico, and the Registro Único Nacional in Bolivia.

by a sequence of governments since the mid-1990s has driven Brazil's remarkable record in achieving near-universal birth registration among children (Hunter & Sugiyama 2018).

A second factor motivating governments in countries such as Colombia and Peru to incorporate more citizens into national identification systems has to do with wanting to reintegrate the population, both socially and politically, in the aftermath of serious internal conflicts. Colombia was wracked by internal violence between the government, paramilitary groups, and the Revolutionary Armed Forces of Colombia (FARC) that began in the 1960s and endured for the better part of the following fifty years. Peru fell victim to the Shining Path and the Túpac Amaru guerrilla groups in the 1980s, powerful insurgencies that lasted into the first half of the 1990s. The governments in both countries recognized that elements of social exclusion lay beneath these movements and the responses to them in the countryside. The drive to build strong national identity systems thereafter no doubt reflected a state interest in being able to know and keep track of the population, but also an interest in incorporating and integrating marginalized individuals into institutions that conferred the benefits and rights of full citizenship. One source writing on Peru labels these imperatives more simply as "security" and "nation building" (Peters & Mawson 2016).

During the height of the violence in both countries, very few people in remote conflict zones were able to register the births of their children. Others lost the documents they had through sheer displacement or intentional destruction (sometimes they even falsified them) because they did not want to be identified by relevant parties in the conflict, including the government. Owing to rebel attacks on government buildings, including civil registry offices (in an era before digital technologies, no less), many individuals lost official records of their civil status and their actual IDs. In both countries, being from an indigenous community and living in a conflict zone (generally in rural areas) had compounding negative effects on registration numbers.

As the violence wound down, the governments in Colombia and Peru sought to make up for lost time and document people who had fallen through the registration cracks as children, many of who were, by then, adults. They also worked to restore official civil status and documents to people who had lost them. Even as far back as 2004, Colombia's civil registry formed a "Unit for Attention to Vulnerable Populations" (UNICEF Innocenti Research Centre 2007, Vengoechea Barrios 2017: 70). Mobile units complete with computers, fingerprint materials, cameras, and satellite antenna to connect up with the national database made their way to isolated mountain regions. The requirement of birth certificates for securing legal identity in Colombia made providing them a key goal of this campaign.[43]

Similarly, in Peru, measures were taken to provide IDs for undocumented children who had fled conflict zones. After these initial measures, the governments in both countries – but with particular success in Peru through the 1993 founding of the National Registry of Identification and Civil Status (RENIEC) – strived to build comprehensive and efficient institutions that brought civil registration functions together with a system for national identity documentation. It is worth mentioning that RENIEC, hailed as a model organization of this type (Peters & Mawson 2016, Reuben & Carbonari 2017), bears the stamp of President Alberto Fujimori (1990–2000). Fujimori was known for overseeing the unfolding of programs (e.g. in health care) characterized as having the double-edged goals of inclusion and control. Notably, RENIEC has partnered with programs in other ministries, namely the Ministry of Development and Social Inclusion, to enable low-income and, for the most part, indigenous Peruvians to gain access to social services. One of the programs it has worked with is JUNTOS, an income-transfer program for poor families.[44]

How Many Latin American and Caribbean Governments Have Made Registration More Accessible

To reach undocumented populations, regardless of the precise combination of motives, governments could not simply do more of the same. If previous civil-registry procedures had resulted in the de facto exclusion of up to 20 percent or so of the population, even as recently as the turn of the century (depending on the precise country in question), governments would need to take extensive proactive measures to "go the last mile." In short, they needed to heighten parents' awareness of the importance of registration and of how to obtain it; reduce the various economic burdens of registration on low-income families; effectively reduce the distance between remote populations and registries; eliminate the intergenerational obstacles to nonregistration; diminish discriminatory practices regarding indigenous language and sociocultural issues; and reduce complications regarding paternity. Decreasing these barriers to birth registration no doubt stimulated higher societal demand than simply

---

[43] Birth certificates are the first step in securing legal identity in Colombia. They are tantamount to proof of nationality for children younger than fourteen years and comprise a foundational document to obtain a national identity card, a citizenship card, and a passport (Vengoechea Barrios 2017: 70).

[44] Excellent sources on Peru include Reuben and Cuenca (2009), RENIEC (2012), Peters and Mawson (2016), Reuben and Carbonari (2017).

introducing benefits alone would have.[45] A brief description of these adminis-trative reforms follows.[46]

- Increasing communication: of the states that had previously failed to explain, in terms understandable to the public, the need and procedures for registering and certifying a birth, many now conduct public information campaigns on the importance of birth registration and how to go about it. They have targeted poor neighborhoods and areas of the country to raise awareness among populations of parents who are not likely to be registered themselves or to register their children. The materials that communicate these messages are often posted in places where people receive public services, such as social welfare offices, health clinics, and schools. The personnel who work in such places are also tasked with getting the word out to vulnerable populations (see, for example, Figure 3).

- Simplifying procedures: of those states in which too many steps were pre-viously necessary to go from recording a live birth to adding it to the civil registry and then undertaking the certification process (with parents having to walk through each step in the sequence on their own), some have tried to link these steps and put bureaucratic agencies in charge of ushering along the process. In countries that still have a significant number of home births, governments have tried to educate and assist midwives in getting the process started by sending records of the live birth to the civil registry. Some countries, such as Bolivia under President Evo Morales, have developed programs to financially incentivize pregnant women to have their babies delivered in clinics instead of in homes, thereby facilitating the process of birth registration (Vidal Fuertes *et al.* 2015).

- Reducing expenses on families: in the states in which the widespread system of semi-private/public notaries had previously charged people excessive fees for birth registration and certification, many governments have begun to subsidize the notaries themselves to eliminate or at least significantly diminish fees for families, as well as reduce petty corruption

---

[45] Many similar reforms were adopted across the region. Beyond being rooted in common impediments to registration, these reforms resulted from intercountry communication among civil registration experts. In addition to UNICEF, Plan International, and the Organization of American States, the Inter-American Development Bank has been an important forum for such communication. An association of Latin American registrars (the Latin American and Caribbean Council for Civil Registration, Identity, and Vital Statistics: CLARCIEV) was also created in 2005 for exchanging ideas on "best practices." For information about this association, see http://clarciev.com/en/

[46] The author has put together an elaborate ranking of countries according to the reforms they have made in this area. Because it is too detailed for the purposes of this Element, readers seeking more information should contact the author.

Figure 3 Brazilian flyer to promote birth registration
Source: https://certidaodenascimento.com.br/certidao-de-nascimento-gratuita/

among registrars. In addition, in the cases where delayed registration had previously carried high costs and logistical complexities, a number of states have issued amnesties for populations that were never registered and have provided a window of opportunity for them to finally do so. Bolivia extended its initial amnesty to all people and later gave an indefinite amnesty to anyone qualifying as indigenous. It is worth mentioning that the task of registering the births of undocumented older people is made easier in Catholic countries owing to the widespread practice of baptism and the baptismal records kept by the church.

- Facilitating access: in the cases where large geographic distances had previously led to a woefully inadequate provision of registrars (adding to economic costs and impeding information about procedural requirements), many states have set up mobile registration units to cover far-reaching areas of the national territory. Moreover, some states have established civil registry outposts at maternity wards[47] and have paid registrars to meet populations at sites of service delivery such as immunization clinics and schools. The basic idea is for the state to reach out to vulnerable populations and bundle registration with essential services.[48]

- Reducing sexism: regarding states where mothers had previously been prohibited from registering children on their own, some Latin American countries have changed the rules and procedures to allow them to now do

---

[47] See Muzzi (2010).
[48] On bundling, see Goodwin and Maru (2014).

so. Since some of the bias was rooted in norms and customs rather than formal rules, some governments have socialized their registrars to become more open to mothers registering their children.

- Reducing the impact of unrecognized paternity: in states where gratuitous registration practices had previously stigmatized children without recognized paternity, state officials are now socialized to be more sensitive to the issue. Institutionally, some of these gratuitous practices have been eliminated, such as the use of the term "illegitimate child" on the birth certificate and making the child take the mother's last name twice in the tradition of two Spanish surnames (e.g. Martínez Martínez), which was tantamount to announcing unclaimed paternity. Some countries have allowed the mother to designate a second last name for the child, generally that of a family member. Moreover, some states have implemented forced DNA testing to establish paternity on a child's birth records.

- Eliminating the intergenerational barrier to registration: in cases where undocumented parents had previously been unable to register their children because they lacked an official identity, many states have put procedures in place that rely on witnesses and other informal means to establish parentage. These witnesses attest to the fact that the people who seek registration are in fact the parents of the child, and that the child is approximately the age that they claim it is. Other countries, for example Brazil, have insisted that the parents be documented themselves but have facilitated registration for undocumented parents.

- Becoming more open to sociocultural and language diversity: among the states in which registration procedures had previously worked to exclude indigenous names and people who did not speak Spanish (or Portuguese), several Latin American countries have taken steps to make the rules, procedures, and norms of civil registration more open and flexible in these respects. Some countries have also trained speakers of indigenous languages to become registrars. Bolivia and Peru have made exceptional strides in this regard.[49]

Many similar reforms were adopted across the region. Some governments, however, have worked harder to go the last mile than others. Brazil, Peru, and Bolivia stand out as regards the policy efforts they have made to facilitate registration for everyone. Brazil and Peru have done so with remarkable success. Bolivia, which faces many challenges – a mountainous geography, a highly indigenous population, constrained economic resources, and a weak state overall – has made significant strides in birth registration, although

---

[49] See, for example, RENIEC (n.d.), RENIEC (2012), and RENIEC (2015).

significant gaps remain.[50] Mexico, a large federal country that has a decentralized system of civil registration, has implemented fewer policy interventions of the kind described above than would be necessary to address lagging registration levels.[51] The interstate variation in registration levels across Mexico is vast, with Chiapas, Guerrero, and Oaxaca lagging far behind many other states (Mercado Asencio & Ortiz Reyes 2014). Paraguay, despite some recent reforms, is ranked at the lower end of the countries in South America that have instituted measures to lift birth-registration rates.[52] The existence of so many unpaid Paraguayan registrars – one indication of weak state professionalization – no doubt contributes to rent-seeking behavior and therefore the exclusion of marginalized groups. In both Mexico and Paraguay, people of indigenous origins are the least likely to be registered.

Conclusion

This section began with the premise that, if lacking documentation bars people from fully realizing their state membership, the obvious solution rests on individuals to come up with evidence of nationality, beginning with a registered birth. In decades and centuries past in Latin America, this was much easier said than done, as the registration procedures in most countries were onerous and effectively available only to people of means who lived in urban areas, who were literate, who commanded the Spanish or Portuguese language, and who were born in institutional settings. When state officials regarded inequality and exclusion as entirely acceptable, almost the natural order of things, and when politicians were less accountable and responsive to these broader publics, the de facto result was low registration rates among the poor, rural, illiterate, and nondominant language-speaking populations. Being born at home and having undocumented parents reinforced other factors that kept people "off the grid." Many of these same factors are prevalent in countries in other regions and lead to the same result.

Today, programs such as conditional cash transfers and noncontributory pensions make it costlier to be without a birth certificate in Latin America than it was even as recently as twenty-five years ago. Put simply, there are more benefits to get that rely on being able to show a documented birth. Where state

---

[50] See Hunter and Brill (2016) for an analysis of birth registration in Bolivia. See also Roca Serrano (2006) and Visión Mundial Bolivia (2008).

[51] On Mexico and birth registration, see UNICEF Mexico and Instituto Nacional de Estadística y Geografía (n.d.), Valdés (2011), Mercado Asencio (2012), and Mercado Asencio and Ortiz Reyes (2014).

[52] On Paraguay and birth registration procedures, see Ordoñez Bustamente (2007), de Servin (2007), Pero Ferreira (2012), and Campos Ojeda *et al.* (2014).

benefits are high but the number of people who are documented is low, an important demand-side opportunity for registration exists. Nonetheless, it takes a determined state to overcome the barriers that kept many people from registering in previous periods. Policy reforms to facilitate registration of the type described above have been necessary to meet the increased demand for documents. Extensions in institutionalized social protection since the 1990s and efforts to reintegrate countries after internal conflicts have thus increased the demand for and supply of birth registration, raising the life chances of the poor and strengthening civil registry systems in the process.

This a political story but also a policy story. The motivations for including a broader swath of the population in the civil registries of countries were largely political, with the broader aim being social inclusion and, in some cases, a combination of inclusion and control. The measures taken to do so come down to effective policymaking. Once political leaders and the states they oversaw made a commitment to broaden inclusion, the policy implications for realizing this result were apparent. It is encouraging that even states with relatively low bureaucratic capacity and financial means (e.g. Bolivia) have been able to achieve a notable degree of progress through a number of strategic interventions. The implication here is that other countries can also advance if state officials wish it. The arguments advanced in this section promise to have broader applicability as welfare states form in other developing regions and/or political elites seek to reintegrate their countries and make their populations legible in the aftermath of civil violence.

This section shed light on the registration procedures that were not specifically intended to exclude marginalized groups but, in effect, exerted a differential impact on segments within the population. The next section turns to situations of evidentiary statelessness that have resulted from the deliberate exclusion of certain ascriptive groups. In these cases, state officials have hidden behind onerous administrative procedures to intentionally keep "the other" from gaining access to coverage and thereby to state membership.

4 Active Denial of Access to Proof of Nationality: Excluding Haitian Descendants in the Dominican Republic and Nubian Descendants in Kenya

This section examines and analyzes two cases of evidentiary statelessness that are the result of intentional state discrimination. There are many others like these in the world. The cases discussed here demonstrate the lengths to which the states of the Dominican Republic and Kenya have gone to exclude minorities from state membership by insisting on documentation that the groups in question inevitably have difficulty producing. These examples from the

Dominican Republic and Kenya go considerably beyond the exclusion experienced by marginalized segments of the population in Latin America, as was
discussed in the previous section. In terms of Figure 2, they fall into the category
of "active denial of access to proof" (of nationality). There are also thousands of
people in these countries (if not millions in Kenya) whose birth was not
registered for reasons of simple marginality, not unlike the situation described
in the previous section. The particular purpose of this section, however, is to
draw attention to those groups that are the targets of intentional discrimination
in these same countries.

Haitian Descendants in the Dominican Republic

The case of the Dominican government against Dominicans of Haitian descent
is interesting. It shows how international pressure against a frontal legal assault
to state membership in the contemporary Western world may cause a country to
shift course and go down the alternative path of generating evidentiary statelessness, although with a very suboptimal result for the people affected. It is
interesting from another angle as well. As a rule, legal statelessness for those
born in the Western Hemisphere is uncommon, largely because of the observa-
tion of birthright citizenship rules. The Dominican Republic is a notable
exception, having shifted from a *jus soli* regime to effectively a *jus sanguinis*
regime (with all the associated evidentiary requirements), which resulted in the
creation of an estimated 200,000 stateless persons of Haitian descent (Price
2017: 30–32). This section will describe and analyze the effort that was required
to make that bold move and the later shift downward that put most Haitian
descendants in a situation of evidentiary statelessness.

By way of background, the marginalization of Haitians in the Dominican
Republic is not a new phenomenon. Tensions date back to the massive
migrations of Haitians into the country as agricultural workers in the 1920s,
when the United States occupied the island. Agreements were signed with
Haiti in 1952, 1959, and 1966 to bring agricultural workers and their families
into the Dominican Republic. The system was designed in such a way that
immigrants had to remain in special zones called "bateyes." The one ID that
Haitians received was a worker identification card, reflecting the importance
of migrant Haitian workers to the Dominican economy. Tensions were especially pronounced during the Great Depression, as many economic elites
pinned the failings of the Dominican economy on Haitian migrants. Ethnic
violence erupted under dictator Rafael Trujillo in the late 1930s, when
he directed the Dominican military to begin a campaign of terror and intimidation against Haitians in the country. This violence resulted in the deaths
of approximately 20,000 Haitian men, women, and children and made

"*antihaitianismo*" official state policy. Even as the Dominican economy recovered, anti-Haitian sentiment proved lasting (American Jewish World Service 2016). More agreements were signed in the 1970s and 1980s owing to the rapid growth of the Dominican sugar economy and an urgent need for workers. A permanent Haitian population was settled in an environment of territorial exclusion. Today, many Dominicans continue to blame Haitians for shortcomings in the country.

The Dominican Constitution of 1929 granted nationality on the *jus soli* principle. It, and all subsequent constitutions up to that of 2010, granted citizenship to "Every person born in the territory of the Dominican Republic, except for the legitimate sons of foreign residents in the Dominican Republic in a diplomatic representation or in transit." The exact terms of "in transit," however, were never clearly defined. Whereas the Inter-American Commission on Human Rights (IACHR) maintains that, based on a 1939 immigration law, "in transit" refers to a period of ten days or fewer, recent Dominican governments have used this ambiguity to retroactively remove nationality rights from all Haitians in the country by alleging that illegal Haitian migrants were all "in transit," even though they may have resided in the Dominican Republic for decades (Comisión Interamericana de Derechos Humanos 2015).

Moreover, this ambiguity is set against a backdrop of a confusing and even corrupt civil registry system run by the Junta Central Electoral (JCE), the Dominican Republic's electoral certification administration. An international commission consisting of Bolivia, Nicaragua, Paraguay, and the Dominican Republic itself detailed the many shortcomings of the pre-2004 JCE. These weaknesses included "excessive formalities and rigidity in administrative procedures," including "unnecessary referral to the judicial sphere" for resolution, "the political appointment of Civil Status Officers," which sets the stage for potential corruption, and "existing legal barriers" to registration "that are in many cases impossible or difficult to satisfy or comply with," even in the most privileged of circumstances (Plan International 2004: 7–8). This report argues that these inhibitory bureaucratic challenges stem from a lack of political will on behalf of the Dominican state to implement smart public policy reform focused on valuing "humans rights and democratic development," including the role of civil registration in securing those objectives. Thus, as of 2004, the international community had already judged that the legal and institutional dysfunctionality surrounding birth registration in the Dominican Republic created the "Haitian problem," namely the fact that hundreds of thousands of undocumented migrant workers have no possibility of acquiring legal status "as foreigners with legal residence" or nationalized foreigners, let alone as Dominicans with completely documented citizenship.

The deliberate erosion of nationality status for Haitians born in the Dominican Republic first reared its head in 2004, when a new migration law (285–2004) replaced a 1939 migration law that (somewhat) defined "in transit" as ten days or fewer. The new law – fully implemented in April, 2007 – would admit people into the country either as "residents" or "nonresidents." The workers (and former workers) that originated from Haiti that were living in the Dominican Republic were classified as nonresidents and the law declared that all nonresidents would be considered "in transit." This law created a gray area of interpretation as to whether *jus soli*-based citizenship still applied to people born in the Dominican Republic after the law passed (from resident or non-resident parents). Furthermore, Article 28 of the law established that new-borns of nonresidents had to be registered in the consulate of their parents' home country, with hospitals in the Dominican Republic registering them with a pink certificate that did not automatically provide state membership. Since the 2002 Constitution did not make provisions for "nonresidents", it became unclear whether *jus soli* or the new migration law would apply.

Up until that moment, the only people who fell into a situation of serious legal ambiguity were the offspring of non-residents born between 1939 and 2004 whose parents stayed in the country for ten days or less. Yet the 2004 law (Article 151) changed this by ordering the creation of a plan to regularize all nonresidents living in the Dominican Republic under the old migration law from the 1930s. It stated explicitly that any children of nonresidents, even children born in the Dominican Republic, would need to report to the consulate of their country of origin for documentation. It was becoming ever clearer that the government was telling Haitian descendants that they did not belong in the country, with earlier, draft versions of this law specifically restricting the obligation to report to a consulate only to Haitians (Plan International 2004: 11). In 2005, the Supreme Court ruled that anyone without a residency permit from the new Migration Direction would be considered "in transit," no matter how long that person had been in the Dominican Republic.

In reaction to this slippage of Dominican nationality among Haitian descendants, the Inter-American Court stated that "although the determination of who is a national of a particular state continues to fall within the ambit of state sovereignty, states' discretion must be limited by international human rights that exist to protect individuals against arbitrary state actions" (Inter-American Court of Human Rights 2005). In what became a well-known move in international legal circles, the Court condemned the Dominican Republic in 2006 for denying late-issued birth certificates to two children of Haitian origin who were born in the Dominican Republic, as were their mothers. This landmark judgment in *Dilcia Yean and Yioleta*

Bosico v. *Dominican Republic* found the Dominican Republic guilty of purposefully misapplying the "in transit" constitutional clause to exclude Haitians of their legal right to claim Dominican nationality. The statement issued by the Court urged the Dominican Republic to recognize "that a foreigner who develops connections in a State cannot be equated to a person in transit" (Open Society Foundations 2010: 6). Furthermore, by using "in transit" as a proxy for determining nationality, the Court found that the Dominican Republic was not only imposing discriminatory effects on Haitians within the country but also making thousands of children vulnerable to statelessness, a violation of international legal agreements.

The government of the Dominican Republic maintained adamantly that it was not violating human rights conventions about nationality rights because Haitian immigrants (and their descendants) had a *jus sanguinis* right to Haitian citizenship. In short, government spokespeople argued that because they could apply for Haitian naturalization (they were not automatically Haitian nationals because the 1987 Haitian Constitution restricted citizenship to children of at least one *native-born* Haitian parent), they did not need Dominican nationality and were not permanently stateless. This stance ignored the fact that many Dominican Haitians had never been to Haiti and therefore had no ties there with which to prove their heritage. In addition, Haiti's civil registry capacity is extremely limited, making it very unlikely that all foreign births could be documented – a process that relies on documentation of the child's parents by Haiti as well (United States Department of State: Bureau of Democracy, Human Rights and Labor 2015: 20, Baluarte 2017: 86–87). Even if those eligible for Haitian naturalization could prove their Haitian descent with formal documentation, for many decades up to 2012, Haiti banned dual nationality and stripped Haitian nationality from those who claimed another, including Dominican (Amnistía Internacional 2015). The Inter-American Court therefore rejected the Dominican Republic's reasoning in *Dilcia Yean and Yioleta Bosico* v. *Dominican Republic*, arguing that the Dominican Republic would effectively be leaving children of Haitian descent born on national territory without a state by conferring the migratory status of their ancestors unduly onto them (Open Society Foundations 2010: 6).

A circular memo, "Circular 017," issued by the government of the Dominican Republic in 2007 proceeded to limit the delivery of birth certificates to the offspring of people in an irregular migratory situation. Circular 017 gave ample discretionary power to civil registrars to determine what constitutes the possibility that birth certificates presented to them for the purpose of accessing other IDs "may have been improperly issued to children of 'foreign parents who had not proven their residency or legal status' " (Open Society Foundations 2010: 11). Using this discretion, registrars could (and do) deny "suspect" certificates on the basis of the presenter being black, not speaking proper Spanish, or having a non-Spanish surname. This circular in effect deprives Dominican nationals of Haitian descent of their legal right to unobstructed access to all of their personal government records. There is no doubt that this policy specifically targets Haitian migrants, as the phrase "foreign parents" has been replaced with "Haitian parents" in some registries' copies of the circular (Open Society Foundations 2010: 11,Amnistía Internacional 2015: 15).

A resolution, "Resolución 12–2007," adds further restrictions to the access that Haitians residing in the Dominican Republic may have to their personal records. It goes a step beyond Circular 017 in authorizing civil registrars to outright suspend, without official review, any state-issued IDs – including the national identity cards that all Dominicans must possess over the age of sixteen years – owing to perceived "irregularities." Less than one year after the issuance of this resolution, the vast majority of the 3,115 IDs that were suspended and under official review by the JCE belonged to people of Haitian origin (Open Society Foundations 2010: 13). The JCE, to this day, remains notorious for its complicated appeals process and its practice of issuing decisions without notice to those they concern. In addition, the hoops that victims of such discrimination must jump through often discourage them from "appealing their effective denationalization," as "many do not wish to engage in additional contact" with the bureaucracy responsible (Open Society Foundations 2010: 14–15). Furthermore, the fact that they lack any form of ID makes any such procedural appeals difficult to begin, even if an appeal was desired by those affected.

The boldest addition to government policies stripping documentation from Haitians in the Dominican Republic came with the ratification of a new con-stitution in 2010. It added a clause stating officially that the offspring of people residing illegally in Dominican territory would be excluded from *jus soli*-based Dominican nationality. In short, the 2010 Constitution took the 2004 migration law one step further toward exclusion by integrating its verbiage directly into the nation's governing document and retroactively stripping citizenship. Therefore – despite the ruling in *Dilcia Yean and Yioleta Bosico* v. *Dominican Republic* – the new constitution makes the acquisition of Dominican nationality for the children of foreigners born in the Dominican Republic entirely depen-dent on their parents' migration status, with those whose parents were consid-ered, at their time of birth, "in transit" effectively unable to claim Dominican citizenship (Open Society Foundations 2010: 16).[53]

---

[53] It should be mentioned that the broader context of 2010 was not favorable for Haitian descen-dants in the Dominican Republic. A major earthquake in Haiti in January, 2010, which claimed upward of 100,000 lives, also led to a serious outbreak of cholera in the country. Subsequent

In 2013, the constitutional tribunal issued a resolution on a specific case (TC-068–2013), denying Dominican nationality to a woman born in the 1960s with a valid birth certificate. Government officials alleged that she was not a citizen in accordance with the new constitution because she was the daughter of immigrants "in transit," understood in the new definition of the 2004 migration law and the 2010 Constitution. This verdict effectively rested on reinterpreting all Dominican migratory policy going back to 1929, establishing that the principle of being in transit had always applied. Notably, the verdict explicitly mentioned that it applied to Haitians. After this 2013 ruling, any descendant from Haitians living in the Dominican Republic lost the right to Dominican nationality. It ordered a review, effectively a repeal, of Dominican citizenship status for this population going back to 1929, putting an estimated 200,000 Dominicans of Haitian descent at risk of statelessness. Without resolution, this would create the largest population of stateless people in the Western Hemisphere, a region internationally recognized for historically low levels of statelessness owing to near-universal national policies of *jus soli*-based citizenship.

This ruling, aimed at full-on denationalization, provoked a major international outcry from various quarters, including the international community and the Dominican diaspora.[54] The UNHCR and IACHR publicly condemned the ruling, and communities of expats began mobilizing protest movements elsewhere, such as the "We Are All Dominican" movement in the United States. The next year (2014), the Dominican government turned away from making people legally stateless and instead devised a plan to either (1) reissue the invalidated preexisting ID(s) of those born before the 2004 law fully took effect in 2007 (Group A) or (2) register as "foreigners" those who never had documents in the first place (Group B) and put them through an exceedingly onerous series of administrative challenges to reapply for Dominican citizenship. Both of these processes could be carried out only in the country's capital city by people with the wherewithal to navigate the system. Moreover, it remains unclear to this day what process, if any, there is for those born in the Dominican Republic between the implementation of the 2004 law (in 2007) and the 2010 constitutional reform (Amnistía Internacional 2015, Human Rights Watch 2015, Dominicanos por Derechos *et al.* 2018: 13). It appears

---

cholera cases confirmed among Haitians who had fled into the Dominican Republic led to public outcry and even less solidarity with Haitian descendants. Notably, however, a lack of documentation among many Haitian descendants made it difficult for them to interact with the public health system and heed the warnings issued by the government, which simply reinforced anti-Haitian sentiments among the population (Keys *et al.* 2017: 12).

[54] For more information on this complex and well-publicized case, see Georgetown Law Human Rights Institute Fact-Finding Project (2013), Amnistía Internacional (2015), Human Rights Watch (2015), International Human Rights Clinic (2015), and Price (2017).

that this new "Naturalization Law" (169–2014), which put many people up against stiff evidentiary challenges, was passed owing to the aforementioned considerable international pressure. The pressure was exacerbated by backlash from the Caribbean Community (CARICOM) – which the Dominican Republic was attempting to join at the time – as well as new domestic organizations voicing active opposition to this arbitrary denationalization (Human Rights Watch 2015: 8).

The new law of 2014 (law 169) divides the population denationalized by the 2013 ruling into two groups: A and B. Group A consists of those born before the post-2004 legal shift and who have Dominican birth certificates in their possession, making those of Haitian descent officially Dominican citizens. However, because of "irregularities" found in their civil registry entries owing to being born of undocumented migrants, these people have needed to "restore" their citizenship and verify their previously issued documents through an application process. Approximately 54,000 people fit into this category. On the other hand, Group B consists of approximately 180,000 Dominican-born individuals of Haitian parentage whose births were never registered, making them "undocumented Haitian migrants" under the law. People in this category needed to register into a book for foreigners within 180 days of the law's passage, obtain a migratory permit, and then complete a two-year naturalization process with stiff requirements, such as sworn, notarized testimony from a midwife or seven witnesses to prove birth within the Dominican Republic. After this period of two years, if all conditions for nationalization were met, those in Group B would have the *opportunity* to be naturalized by presidential decree – clearly by no means a guarantee (Human Rights Watch 2015: 12–13).

Adding another twist to this process is the fact that, under Dominican law, registering as a foreigner requires that a foreign identification document be produced. Hardly any of the applicants in this group would logically possess a foreign ID, such as a Haitian passport, because they are Dominican nationals and not nationals of any other country (Human Rights Watch 2015: 24). Therefore, the mere act of requiring people to register as foreigners within their own country using foreign IDs when they have no other nationality creates a virtually impossible scenario. If, after all this, those in Group B were found ineligible for naturalization at the end of the two-year process, they were left with little recourse.

According to the IACHR, by 2016, only about 8,000 of the roughly 180,000 people in Group B had taken the steps necessary to attempt to (re)obtain Dominican citizenship. Time constraints, prohibitive costs (nearly US$400), and administrative complications within the JCE and the Ministry of Interior and Police (which was given oversight of Group B) hindered most from applying, let alone successfully completing the arduous process. The term to register expired in mid-2015 and so, except for the approximately 750 Dominican Haitians who received residency permits prior to the application period closing, the rest of Group B, as well as those born between the implementation of the 2004 law (in 2007) and the 2010 constitutional reform, remains in legal limbo (United States Department of State 2015: 23).

A case challenging the terms of the new law quickly came before the Inter-American Court of Human Rights in late 2014. In *Expelled Dominicans and Haitians* v. *Dominican Republic*, the Inter-American Court found the Dominican Republic to be in violation of international law concerning statelessness and human rights, including the 1961 Convention to Reduce Cases of Statelessness (which the Dominican Republic has not ratified) and eleven articles of the 1969 American Convention on Human Rights, to which it is a signatory. The Court pointed out specific violations of Article 20 of the Convention, which states:

1. Every person has the right to a nationality.
2. Every person has the right to the nationality of the state in whose territory he was born if he does not have the right to any other nationality.
3. No one shall be arbitrarily deprived of his nationality or of the right to change it.

This finding aligns with the view of the UNHCR that the 2013 Dominican Supreme Court ruling backdating the "in transit" clause made the status of those affected an issue of legal statelessness. Furthermore, it conforms to the view that nationality is determined from the moment it is assessed, "not based on theoretical future applications for citizenship that may or may not be granted" (Georgetown Law Human Rights Institute Fact-Finding Project 2013: 43–45). Therefore, the 2014 ruling held that the Dominican Republic faces an obligation to grant nationality to all those born within its territory who are stateless or are at "risk of statelessness," as is the case for the hundreds of thousands of children of Haitian migrants born in the country without documentation. The statement reiterated that naturalization is not the same thing as nationalization and that the Dominican Republic's plan for Group B erred legally in that respect as well. For its part, the Dominican Republic has (predictably) rejected this ruling by the Inter-American Court as one trampling on national sovereignty and overstepping jurisdiction. It quickly withdrew from the convention and from public commitment to international human rights protocols.

The main point to be made here is that the Dominican Republic is technically on the right side of international law because, by the strict terms of the 2014 law, those in Group A and those in Group B could obtain citizenship in principle and therefore are not stateless. However, the costs, evidence, and legal assistance necessary to do so exceeded what most in Group B (and some in Group A) could muster. The 2014 revision to the initial 2013 Supreme Court ruling therefore offers no real solution for the largest group involved, those who were born in the Dominican Republic to parents without legal residence and who cannot prove their birthplace or produce any parental identification documents.[55] These people are at risk of being deported. Indeed, after the initial deadline for registration passed in 2015, at least 58,271 Haitians who failed to make the cut-off were forcibly deported and at least 70,000 more fled to makeshift, unsanitary refugee settlements across the Haitian border due to fear of violence or intimidation (Ahmed 2015, Dominicanos por Derechos *et al.* 2018: 12). These deportations followed those of thousands of other illegal Haitian migrants in early 2015 under a government plan called *Operación Escudo* (Operation Shield), which occasionally swept up some people in Group B who had started or attempted to start registration on time and were supposedly protected from deportation during that process (Human Rights Watch 2015: 29–30).

Group B's counterparts in Group A – who tended to be more affluent, integrated, and better positioned to hire legal assistance – started the process of naturalization with the advantage conferred by a document that certifies their births in the Dominican Republic.[56]

The post-2014 system thus leaves out the most marginalized of Dominican society. Although human rights institutions (such as the IACHR and bodies associated with the UN) have contested the situation, thousands of people still fall short of realizing full Dominican nationality owing to a lack of evidence. Now mass deportations are no longer occurring and with those negatively affected having little ability to obtain legal counsel or induce the media to lobby their cases, the Dominican Republic is out of the international "dog house" and off the front-page news (United States Department of State 2015: 15).

Although the crisis may be over (as Haitian descendants no longer qualify as *officially* stateless), the chronic situation of marginalization for those in Group B

---

[55] Some legal scholars have expressed consternation with the 2014 ruling. For example, David C. Baluarte of the Washington and Lee School of Law maintains that, based strictly on the ruling, the Dominican Republic appears to be in compliance with international law and that Haitian descendants are not officially stateless (Baluarte 2017: 78–80, 88, 90–92). He claims that the Court's extension of the stateless classification to those more appropriately considered "at risk" of statelessness might actually leave such people less protected.

[56] Individuals in Group A, however, have not gone through the process entirely without violations of their citizenship rights. The Human Rights Watch reported in 2015 that at least 120 original nationality documents filed for the Group-A process had been arbitrarily suspended "pending review" or had been declared outright invalid by the JCE (Human Rights Watch 2015: 16–19).

in particular continues. In November, 2017, the Dominican Republic stated to the IACHR that "it was not aware of any application for naturalization filed by any of the population registered as Group B," even though some applicants should have by then been well past the two-year waiting period (Dominicanos por Derechos *et al.* 2018: 12). Having to pay bribes to the police and other state authorities to remain out of trouble for being undocumented is among the many practical reasons that this state of limbo needs to be resolved. Another issue has to do with schooling. In fact, many public schools in the Dominican Republic, especially at the secondary level, discriminate against applicants without official papers. Moreover, evidence suggests that there are deleterious effects for public health. Not having a registered birth in the Dominican Republic reduces the probability that children will complete the required childhood immunizations (Corbacho *et al.* 2013). This is because such children cannot be registered in the social security system, which guarantees access to public vaccination facilities or reimburses charges incurred in private health institutions. The nonimmunization of large numbers of people in a population does not make for a healthy state of affairs. Nor does making it difficult for segments of the population to interact with the public health system in crises such as the cholera epidemic of 2010 (Keys *et al.* 2017). Other issues, such as access to formal employment, exploitation of labor and sex, disenfranchisement, and an inability to register the future children of undocumented migrants, are among the many other aspects of life that are negatively affected by the Dominican Republic's citizenship policies (Amnistía Internacional 2015). The situation of intergenerational stateless-ness imposed upon Haitian descendants in the Dominican Republic thus has both individual and collective costs.

Nubians in Kenya

Across the world, another situation of evidentiary statelessness has long existed. By way of introduction, Kenya has a *jus sanguinis* basis of citizenship and forty-two official ethnic groups. If a person is from one of the forty-two tribes of the country, he or she is assumed to be Kenyan. The Nubians are not one of the favored tribes, even though they have lived in the country for well over a century. In fact, relocated by force by the British Colonial Administration from Sudan, they first arrived in Kenya in the late nineteenth century. Their identification with the colonizing power has given them long-term "enemy" status (Blitz 2009: 10). The rules of nationality at the time of Kenya's indepen-dence in 1963 conferred on them a legal claim to Kenyan nationality, although few of them obtained Kenyan documents. Their struggle against evidentiary statelessness has continued ever since. The overwhelming majority of Nubians identify strongly as Kenyans (Balaton-Chrimes 2016). Well over 99 percent say they are Kenyan and 99 percent also regard their parents as Kenyans. Moreover, there is no other conceivable state (including the Sudan) to which they would want to belong and that would want them. At the same time, however, Nubians are still viewed by many, including Kenyan state officials, as foreigners from the Sudan. Not regarded by the state as integral to Kenya's ethnic makeup, the Nubians were not even counted in national censuses until 2009. In the words of one author, "Perhaps the only consistency in the Nubians' story is their status as in-between or outside the categories that dictate, in formal and informal terms, belonging in the communities in which they found themselves (Balaton-Chrimes 2016: 149).

The core original settlement of the Nubians is what is now the extensive Kibera slum in Nairobi. With a population that could be as large as 500,000, Kibera is often regarded as the biggest urban slum in Africa. Today, about 50 percent of the Nubian community in Kenya resides in and around Kibera. Although they reside in the capital city of a major country, the Nubians have faced stiff challenges in becoming documented. For example, it is estimated that 37 percent of Nubians do not have a birth certificate. Only 87 percent ultimately are successful in obtaining a national identity card and to do so they often have to pay bribes. One conservative estimate is that at least 13 percent of Nubian adults are stateless, defined in evidentiary terms (Open Society Justice Initiative 2011b). Many older people in particular have no identification whatsoever.[57] Their undocumented lives typically began with being born at home. One of the worst consequences of not securing a national ID is the resulting lack of access to the Kenyan National Hospital Insurance Fund and National Social Security Fund.

Besides the core historic reason for discriminating against the Nubians (their association with the colonial power), another reason has become highly relevant in contemporary times: the Nubians are Muslim, unlike the majority of Kenyans. Islam is a fundamental aspect of Nubian identity. In the aftermath of a series of dramatic attacks by Somali terrorist organizations in Kenya, including al-Shabaab's well-known assault on the upscale Westgate shopping mall in 2013, Kenyan officials and society alike seem to be coming up with new reasons to discriminate against groups that were historically excluded for other reasons.[58] Whereas British collaboration was the old

---

[57] This information about extreme documentary deficiencies among Nubian elders was obtained in an author interview with paralegals Makkah Yusuf and Zahra Khalid Osman of the Nubian Rights Forum in Nairobi on July 13, 2017.

[58] On the Kenyan state's fear of Somali identity, see Burbidge (2015).

frame, state security is the new frame for Nubians being suspected. However, rather than issue a major ruling that blocks Nubians collectively and frontally from obtaining Kenyan nationality, to which they have a right under the laws governing independence and in the most recent constitution (2010), the Kenyan state has allowed and even sanctioned registrars to subject Nubians as individuals to vetting procedures. In effect, the central state delegates the authority to exclude to bureaucrats below it.

Vetting is administrative, not statutory.[59] There seem to be few rules governing who gets to be a registrar and what is "fair game" for them to ask. The highly discretionary process of vetting puts many Nubians in a gray zone between statelessness and citizenship. Having a Muslim name appears to work against people. Asking for the documents of people's ancestors, which were arbitrarily denied to previous generations of Nubians, is a common basis for effectively denying present-day Nubians the national ID that essentially confers nationality.[60] Given that having one Kenyan parent confers nationality, on the surface, asking for parents' documentation seems neutral enough, but such a request has a disparate impact on Nubians and groups like them. In accordance with a secret government circular (dated 2007), it was deemed legitimate to ask Nubians and select minorities that live on the border, as well as coastal Arabs and South Asians (many of whom are Muslim), for their grandparents' birth and death certificates and for their title deeds (Makoloo 2005, Sing'oei 2009, Balaton-Crimes 2014, Namati 2014, 2015, Open Society Justice Initiative, the Open Society Initiative for East Africa, Namati, and the Nubian Rights Forum 2014). Being from an ethnic Somali group is also a recipe for nationality denial. When asked, registrars have even admitted that for "nonindigenous Kenyans," they asked for extra birth certificates, including of parents and grandparents (Balaton-Crimes 2014). Among Nubians, 44 percent report having been vetted when applying for an identity card. This approach is part of a pattern of ethnic discrimination that can be seen in many postcolonial African states.

Not having a registered birth and the corresponding certificate has also kept many Nubian children out of school, despite laws about the universal right to a primary school education. Since vetting takes place only at certain intervals (generally twice a year), children can miss a whole year of school if they didn't get approved in time. If undocumented children are fortunate

---

[59] According to Kenyan human rights lawyer Edwin Abuya, vetting does not have a formal place in Kenyan law but it is not illegal. This came out in an interview with the author in Nairobi on July 12, 2017.

[60] Notably, the application form for the ID still requests information on one's tribe.

enough to reach secondary school, they can face difficulties in sitting their exams. In 2009, the Kenyan government introduced a measure that made having a birth certificate a mandatory requirement in registering for national exams and thereby in obtaining school qualification certificates (Apland *et al.* 2014: 42–44). Given that the birth-registration rate among Nubians is only about 63 percent, full enforcement of this policy would have quite an exclusionary result. Not having a national ID (the ticket to voting) has kept many Nubians out of the electoral process and from having formal sector jobs. It has also kept many from receiving a passport, which many Kenyans seek to gain better paid employment in parts of the Middle East (Open Society Justice Initiative *et al.* 2014).

Figure 4, which comes from the Open Society Justice Initiative (2011b) is illustrative in showing the relationship among discrimination, documents, and statelessness.

In this light, when comparing the situation of evidentiary statelessness experienced by Haitian descendants and Nubians with that of low-income, rural, indigenous Latin Americans in the previous section, the situation of overt discrimination with no apparent state will to promote greater inclusion puts the former in an arguably more difficult situation than the latter. Given that discrimination is coming from the state itself (and is being implemented at the local level by state agents, who have ample discretion toward applicants), evidentiary hurdles are arguably much harder to overcome. In addition, the fact that the discrimination is the result not of a single ruling (which could be overturned legally) but of fragmented street-level decision-making makes it difficult for the legal community to challenge. Setting bribery aside or the occasional possibility that a (likely more educated, more resourceful) Nubian is able to navigate his or her case through the administrative maze, jumping over these hurdles generally involves enlisting help from outside the exclusionary system.

One solution that is receiving more and more attention is the use of community paralegals who are associated with NGOs to push people's cases through the system. Since Nubians and many other ethnic groups do have a legal claim to Kenyan citizenship, there is in fact a basis upon which documents can be obtained. The paralegal route, which is within the financial means of many Nubians, seems to have had an empowering effect on them. At a basic level, paralegals help people understand and navigate the system that affects them. Paralegals have helped their Nubian clients to arrange papers and prepare their cases, and have accompanied them to meetings with registrars. Notably, when paralegals are present, registrars seem to ask for less outrageous evidence, not to mention fewer bribes and

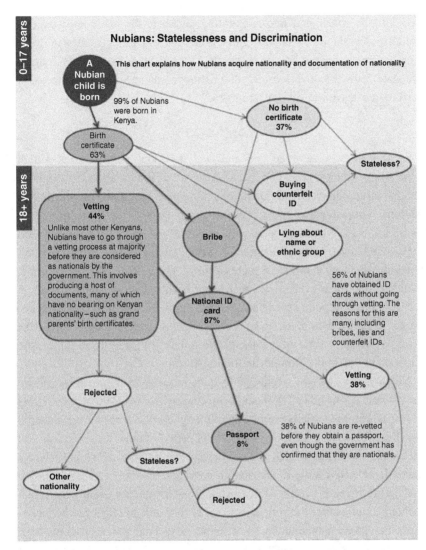

Figure 4 Nubians: statelessness and discrimination

Source: Open Society Justice Initiative (2011b). The Open Society Foundations IP Grant gave print and electronic permissions for reproduction of the work.

lower payments for miscellaneous costs such as photocopying.[61] In short, the likelihood of giving people the "run around" is reduced. Paralegals have also started to run mobile registration drives in Kibera to get ahead of the problem and register the births of young children. Such registration

---

[61] This information was obtained in an author interview with paralegals Makkah Yusuf and Zahra Khalid Osman of the Nubian Rights Forum in Nairobi on July 13, 2017.

may still be considered late registration, but it is far better than waiting until after childhood (Nubian Rights Forum 2018). Paralegal assistance is a stop-gap measure, but is a measure that should be considered as long as the state refuses to oversee the administrative changes necessary to allow for broader access to the civil registry.[62]

Conclusion

This section has examined and analyzed the more nefarious version of evidentiary statelessness. For illustrations, it has drawn upon the plight of Haitian descendants in the Dominican Republic and Kenyans of Nubian descent. Long-standing prejudice exists against both of these groups in their countries. Notably, the spoken reasons for bias toward the Nubians have evolved from their historical collaboration with the British to their potential to form a threat to state security given their Muslim religion. Notably, albeit less pronounced than other biasing factors, state officials in the Dominican Republic have been quick to deride Haitian descendants based on factors related to diseases such as cholera and more recently the Zika virus, which have little relevance for those they are trying to exclude, who have long lived in the Dominican Republic.

Notably, the basis of exclusion in both cases is to try to deny official recognition of "the other." Without documents, neither the Haitian descendants nor the Nubians are able to exercise their full rights as citizens or receive the full benefits of citizenship. Although, for a brief period of time, the government of the Dominican Republic tried to denationalize Haitian descendants entirely in a dramatic collective way, it was able to achieve a similar result of exclusion without incurring the wrath of international public opinion, simply by implementing requirements for proving nationality that were too high for the individuals they were targeting. In short, rather than hold out for full-on legal deprivation of state membership and engage in "overreach," it was sufficient to shift downward onto the terrain of "administrative denial of nationality." It would not be surprising if other states that have received international criticism for their stateless populations follow suit as time goes on.

Since the fundamental basis of exclusion in these and related cases is political and social, the whole discussion of implementing administrative measures to facilitate the incorporation of the previously excluded is less relevant. Haitian descendants are excluded, as are Nubians, because the state and its agents want them to be. The problem is not one of logistics or state capacity. It is worth

---

[62] https://namati.org/wp-content/uploads/2015/02/What-is-a-Community-Paralegal.pdf. See also Goodwin and Maru (2014) and Maru and Gauri (2018).

pointing out, however, that a person is always better off with feeder documents than without them. Haitian descendants in the Dominican Republic who can present a Dominican birth certificate to the authorities are in an infinitely better position to regain Dominican nationality status than those without a registered birth. Similarly, the Nubians who have been able to navigate their cases through the system tend to be those who are armed with official proof of their parents' existence in the country at the time of independence. In short, even in the face of strong official animus, documents can serve as powerful protectors in situations in which people are vulnerable.

5 Conclusion

The overriding purpose of this Cambridge Element is to "get the word out" on an issue that has flown largely under the radar of the political science community. Undocumented nationality, also referred to as evidentiary statelessness, is an underappreciated phenomenon that leads to widespread human deprivation in the modern world. Although expert communities in areas ranging from public health to legal studies have long recognized the in-between status of undocumented nationals and the problems suffered by them in accessing the rights and benefits of full citizenship, political scientists and many otherwise-informed people have little familiarity with the matter. In any event, they certainly do not recognize the extent of the problem and its consequences. Full-on statelessness and long-term irregular status in a country have received more attention than undocumented nationality not only in academic political science, but also in the popular media.

Similarly, attention to issues of biometric identification and digital technologies is increasing. Certainly, these technologies can help put millions of people into a unified database, which can help to achieve various goals such as carrying out mass elections, distributing subsidies, and running huge welfare schemes. India's Aadhaar, the world's largest biometric ID system, is but one example of a program that has been the subject of many news stories. Yet, for all the interest stimulated by such high technology developments, the simple fact of birth registration still plays an essential prior role in the establishment of a legal identity for children. Most countries that have achieved universal registration did so with fairly simple means, beginning with ink and paper and moving to computers. In any event, having a biometric identity does not replace being entered into the civil registry of a country – and possessing proof of this event in the form of a birth certificate – to ensure full state membership. This Element has sought to reemphasize the basic matter of civil registration and certification and to illustrate the various causes or reasons why people lack registration and the nationality-granting documents that correspond to registration, including in the United States.

This Element has also tried to demonstrate the consequences of full documentation and how crucial it is to people's ability to navigate bureaucracies in their own countries and abroad. Given that tensions always exist over how to spend public resources, some might downplay the need for official papers, arguing that no one ever died because they lacked a birth certificate. On the contrary, on an individual level, if a birth certificate is necessary to receive services such as essential childhood immunizations and other services vital to health and welfare, premature death may be the result of not being registered. On a collective level, if a state cannot conduct good epidemiological studies on the causes of childhood mortality because it lacks accurate data on how many babies were born in the first place, public health could be compromised.

Some of the factors explaining high rates of registration are modernization and general state capacity. But these are not the whole story. For example, modern middle-income countries with decent state capacity, such as Brazil and Mexico, have left large numbers of people outside their civil registries until recently. By the same token, some less developed, lower income countries (e.g. Peru) have proven capable of lifting their registration rates rather dramatically over a short period of time. Indeed, politics plays an important role in whether the state and its leadership seeks to include everyone in the civil registry or not. Going the last mile is hard because most people who were included earlier were easier to include. If governments seek broad inclusion, there is an important role for policy, namely for interventions that facilitate registration access to even the most isolated and marginalized citizens. In short, in non-compulsory systems, ordinary citizens have to want documents (i.e. they need to perceive concrete benefits that stem from such documents) and states have to have an interest in and strategy for making them widely available. That is the story told in Section 3 to explain the rise in documentation in Latin America over the last twenty years.

If these conditions hold, expert assistance and economic resources by international organizations and NGOs are available. UNICEF, Plan International, the international development banks, and NGOs such as World Vision have a keen interest in promoting universal birth registration. Yet, in the final analysis, states decide who gets to be a fully fledged citizen. If a state wants to exclude people from certain groups from obtaining nationality-granting documents, its ability to do so is formidable. Thus, whether the recent positive experiences of Latin America in going the last mile (outlined in Section 3) will extend to areas with entrenched discrimination (as shown in Section 4 with respect to the Dominican Republic and Kenya) remains in question. In the event that governments are determined to exclude people, the international political zeitgeist leans increasingly in favor of a less visible form of discrimination, that is, administrative instead of legal exclusion. That explains why the Dominican Republic moved from trying to go down the path of legally based denationalization to administratively based exclusion. The end result was the same – weakening the standing of Haitian descendants – but it did not find itself in egregious violation of international law. It also explains why the Kenyan state makes recourse to "vetting," which pushes decisions downward to street-level bureaucrats and thereby deflects attention and blame away from the central state.

Political will is central to enrolling all citizens into the civil registry and providing them with documentary proof that this has occurred. It will thus be interesting to see whether the heightened attention to birth registration in contemporary international campaigns against statelessness, as well as the inclusion of birth registration among the Sustainable Development Goals, will be effective in pushing countries further along the path toward complete registration. It will also be interesting to see whether this will include those countries known for intentional discrimination against certain groups. At stake is whether or not undocumented nationals can move from the ambiguous gray zone that they have inhabited until now to the clearer terrain of fully fledged citizenship, gaining all the benefits and rights that go along with that shift.

References

Adjami, M. (2016). *Statelessness and Nationality in Côte d'Ivoire*, Geneva: UNHCR.

Ahmed, A. (2015). Haitian workers facing deportation by Dominican neighbors. *The New York Times*. Available from: www.nytimes.com/2015/06/17/world/americas/migrant-workers-in-dominican-republic-most-of-them-haitian-face-deportation.html (accessed September 10, 2016).

American Jewish World Service (2016). *Background: A Citizenship Crisis in the Dominican Republic*, New York: American Jewish World Service. Available from: https://ajws.org/who-we-are/resources/background-citizenship-crisis-dominican-republic/ (accessed March 16, 2018).

Amnistía Internacional (2015). *"Sin Papeles No Soy Nadie": Personas Apátridas en al República Dominicana*, Madrid: Amnistía Internacional.

Apland, K., Blitz, B. K., Hamilton, C., Lagaay, M., Lakshman, R., & Yarrow, E. (2014). *Birth Registration and Children's Rights: A Complex Story*, Woking, UK: Plan International.

Arasindo & Partners (2012). Indonesian birth certifications. Available from: www.arasindo.com/index.php/pengadilan-indonesia/akta-kelahiran-indonesia (accessed October 12, 2018).

Bah, A. B. (2017). *Seeking Democracy in Côte d'Ivoire: Overcoming Exclusionary Citizenship*, Ottawa: Global Centre for Pluralism.

Balaton-Chrimes, S. (2014). Statelessness, identity cards and citizenship as status in the case of the Nubians of Kenya. *Citizenship Studies*, 18, 15–18.

Balaton-Chrimes, S. (2016). The Nubians of Kenya: Citizenship in the Gaps and Margins. In E. Hunter, ed., *Citizenship, Belonging, and Political Community in Africa*, Athens, OH: Ohio University Press, pp. 149–178.

Baluarte, D. C. (2017). The risk of statelessness: reasserting a rule for the protection of the right to nationality. *Yale Human Rights and Development Journal*, 19(1), 47–94.

Barany, Z. (2002). *The East European Gypsies: Regime Change, Marginality, and Ethnopolitics*, New York: Cambridge University Press.

Bhabha, J. (2017). The Politics of Evidence: Roma Citizenship Deficits in Europe. In B. N. Lawrance & J. Stevens, eds., *Citizenship in Question: Evidentiary Birthright and Statelessness*, Durham and London: Duke University Press, pp. 43–59.

Bhatia, A., Ferreira, L. Z., Barros, A. J. D., & Victora, C. G. (2017). Who and where are the uncounted children? Inequalities in birth certificate coverage among children under five years in 94 countries using nationally representative household surveys. *International Journal for Equity in Health*, 16(148), 1–11.

Blitz, B. K. (2009). *Statelessness, Protection, and Equality*, Forced Migration Policy Briefing 3, Oxford, UK: University of Oxford, Refugee Studies Centre.

Blitz, B. K. & Lynch, M. eds. (2012). *Statelessness and Citizenship: A Comparative Study on the Benefits of Nationality*, Cheltenham, UK: Edward Elgar Publishing.

Bradley, P. M. (2017). The invisibles: The cruel Catch-22 of being poor with no ID. *The Washington Post*. Available from: www.washingtonpost.com/life style/magazine/what-happens-to-people-who-cant-prove-who-they-are /2017/06/14/fc0aaca2-4215-11e7-adba-394ee67a7582_story.html?utm_ term=.69780b028c0c (accessed September 5, 2017).

Breckenridge, K. & Szreter, S. eds. (2012). *Registration and Recognition*, Oxford, UK: Oxford University Press.

Brennan Center for Justice (2006). *Citizens Without Proof*, New York: NYU School of Law.

Burbidge, D. (2015). The Kenyan state's fear of Somali identity. *Accord*. Available from: https://accord.org.za/conflict-trends/the-kenyan-states-fear-of-somali-identity/ (accessed October 31, 2018).

Buvinic, M. & Carey, E. (2019). *Leaving No One Behind: CRVS, Gender and the SDGs*, Ottawa: International Development Research Centre.

Campos Ojeda, C. D., Benítez Almada, F. Y., & Rotela Zarate, C. G. (2014). *Manual instructivo para Oficiales y postulantes*, Asunción, Paraguay: Civil Registry of Paraguay in cooperation with GIZ (Gesellschaft fur Internationale Zusammenarbeit).

Comisión Interamericana de Derechos Humanos (CIDH) (2015). *Informe sobre la situación de los derechos humanos en la República Dominicana*, Washington, DC: CIDH.

Clapton, G. (2014). The birth certificate, "father unknown" and adoption. *Adoption & Fostering*, 38(3), 209–222.

Corbacho, A. & Rivas, R. O. (2012). *Travelling the Distance*, Working Paper, Washington, DC: Inter-American Development Bank.

Corbacho, A., Brito, S., & Rivas, R. O. (2013). *Does Birth Under-registration Reduce Childhood Immunization?: Evidence from the Dominican Republic*, Working Paper Series 448, Washington, DC: Inter-American Development Bank.

Diaz, J. & Fogel, B. (2019). *Unidentified: How Kids Can Age Out of Texas Foster Care Without Documentation*, Austin, TX: Texas Standard.

Dominicanos por Derechos, Institute on Statelessness and Inclusion, & Center for Justice and International Law (2018). Joint Submission to the Human Rights Council at the 32nd Session of the Universal Periodic Review. Available from: https://uprdoc.ohchr.org/uprweb/downloadfile.aspx?filename=6225&file=EnglishTranslation (accessed February 13, 2019).

Duff, P., Kusumaningrum, S., & Stark, L. (2016). Barriers to birth registration in Indonesia. *The Lancet Global Health*, 4(4), 234–235.

Dunning, C., Gelb, A., & Raghavan, S. (2014). *Birth Registration, Legal Identity, and the Post-2015 Agenda*, Policy Paper 046, Washington, DC: Center for Global Development.

European Roma Rights Centre (ERRC) (2017). *Roma Belong: Statelessness, Discrimination and Marginalisation of Roma in the Western Balkans and Ukraine*, Budapest: ERRC.

Fagernäs, S. (2014). Papers, please! The effect of birth registration on child labor and education in early 20th century USA. *Explorations in Economic History*, 52, 63–92.

Federación Internacional de Administradoras de Fondos de Pensiones (FIAP) (2011). *Noncontributory Pension Programmes*, Santiago: FIAP.

Fleck, G. & Rughinis, C. (2008). *Come Closer: Inclusion and Exclusion of Roma in Present-Day Romanian Society*, Bucharest: Human Dynamics.

Foucault, M. (2007). *Security, Territory, Population*, New York: Palgrave Macmillan.

Gelb, A. (2015). Labor pains: birth and civil registration in Indonesia. *Center for Global Development*. Available from: www.cgdev.org/blog/labor-pains-birth-and-civil-registration-indonesia (accessed December 4, 2017).

Gelb, A. & Metz, A. D. (2018). *Identification Revolution: Can Digital ID Be Harnessed for Development?*, Washington, DC: Center for Global Development.

Georgetown Law Human Rights Institute Fact-Finding Project (2013). *Left Behind: How Stateless in the Dominican Republic Limits Children's Access to Education*, Washington, DC: Georgetown University Law Center.

Goodwin, L. & Maru, V. (2014). *What Do We Know about Legal Empowerment: Mapping the Evidence*, Working Paper, Washington, DC: Namati.

Granillo, A. (2014). Navajos born at home find it hard to get delayed birth certificates. *Knau*. Available from: www.knau.org/post/navajos-born-home-find-it-hard-get-delayed-birth-certificates (accessed September 24, 2018).

Haggard, S. & Kaufman, R. R. (2008). *Development, Democracy, and Welfare States: Latin America, East Asia, and Eastern Europe*, Princeton, NJ: Princeton University Press.

Hammar, T. ed. (1985). *European Immigration Policy: A Comparative Study*, Cambridge, UK: Cambridge University Press.

Hammer, T. (1990). *Democracy and the Nation State*, Aldershot, UK: Avebury.

Harbitz, M. (2013). *The Civil Registry: A Neglected Dimension of International Development*, Technical Note, Washington, DC: Inter-American Development Bank.

Harbitz, M. & Tamargo, M. C. (2009). *The Significance of Legal Identity in Situations of Poverty and Social Exclusion*, Technical Note, Washington, DC: Inter-American Development Bank.

HelpAge International (2011). *Pension Watch: Challenges and Opportunities for Age Verification in Low- and Middle-Income Countries*, Briefing, London: HelpAge International.

Huber, E. & Stephens, J. D. (2012). *Democracy and the Left: Social Policy and Inequality in Latin America*, Chicago: The University of Chicago Press.

Human Rights Watch (2015). *Somos Dominicanos, Somos Dominicanas: Privación arbitraria de la nacionalidad en la República Domincana*, New York: Human Rights Watch.

Hunter, W. (2019). Identity documents, welfare enhancement, and group empowerment in the Global South. *The Journal of Development Studies*, 55(3), 366–383.

Hunter, W. & Brill, R. (2016). "Documents, please:" advances in social protection and birth certification in the developing world. *World Politics*, 68(2), 191–228.

Hunter, W. & Sugiyama, N. B. (2018). Making the newest citizens: the quest for universal birth registration in contemporary Brazil. *The Journal of Development Studies*, 54(3), 397–412.

Inter-American Court of Human Rights. (2005). *Dilcia Yean and Violeta Bosico v. Dominican Republic*, Case No. 12.189.

International Human Rights Clinic (2015). *Justice Derailed: The Uncertain Fate of Haitian Migrants and Dominicans of Haitian Descent in the Dominican Republic*, Baltimore, MD: Johns Hopkins School of Advanced International Studies.

Keys, H. M., Kaiser, B. N., Foster, J. W., Freeman, M. C., Stephenson, R. A., Lund, A. J., & Kohrt, B. A. (2017). Cholera control and anti-Haitian stigma in the Dominican Republic: from migration policy to lived experience. *Anthropology & Medicine*, 23, 1–19.

Kurth, J. & Roelofs, T. (2017). Poor in Michigan with no ID. "I am somebody. I just can't prove it." *Bridge*. Available from: www.bridgemi.com/detroit-journalism-cooperative/poor-michigan-no-id-i-am-somebody-i-just-cant-prove-it (accessed January 23, 2018).

Landrum, S. (2015). From Family Bibles to Birth Certificates: Young People, Proof of Age, and American Political Cultures, 1820–1915. In C. T. Field & N. L. Syrett, eds., *Age In America: The Colonial Era to the Present*, New York: New York University Press, pp. 124–147.

Lawrance, B. N. & Stephens, J. eds. (2017). *Citizenship in Question: Evidentiary Birthrights and Statelessness*, Durham and London: Duke University Press.

Lubrano, A. (2014). For many Americans obtaining a birth certificate proves challenging. *Face to Face*. Available from: http://facetofacegermantown.org/news/many-americans-obtaining-birth-certificate-proves-challenging-alfred-lubrano-inquirer-staff-writer/ (accessed September 27, 2018).

Madrid, R.L. (2012). *The Rise of Ethnic Politics in Latin America*, New York: Cambridge University Press.

Makoloo, M. O. (2005). *Kenya: Minorities, Indigenous Peoples and Ethnic Diversity*, London: Minority Rights Group International.

Manby, B. (2017). "Legal Identity for All" and Childhood Statelessness. In *The World's Stateless Children*, Oisterwijk, the Netherlands: Wolf Legal Publishers (WLP), pp. 313–326.

Maru, V. & Gauri, V. eds. (2018). *Bringing Law to Life: Community Paralegals and the Pursuit of Justice*, New York: Cambridge University Press.

McGuire, J. (2010). *Wealth, Health, and Democracy in East Asia and Latin America*, New York: Cambridge University Press.

Mercado Asencio, K. (2012). The under-registration of births in Mexico: consequences for children, adults, and migrants. *Migration Policy Institute*. Available from: www.migrationpolicy.org/article/under-registration-births-mexico-consequences-children-adults-and-migrants (accessed October 1, 2018).

Mercado Asencio, K. & Ortiz Reyes, O. I. (2014). *El Derecho a la Identidad y la expedición de actas de nacimiento extemporáneas en los Estados de Oaxaca, Guerrero y Chiapas, México*, Mexico City: Woodrow Wilson International Center for Scholars.

Mikkelsen, L., Lopez, A., & Phillips, D. (2015). Why birth and death registration really are "vital" statistics for development. *United Nations Development Programme*. Available from: http://hdr.undp.org/en/content/why-birth-and-death-registration-really-are-%E2%80%9Cvital%E2%80%9D-statistics-development (accessed September 24, 2018).

Muzzi, M. (2010). *UNICEF Good Practices in Integrating Birth Registration into Health Systems (2000–2009)*, Working Paper, New York: UNICEF.

Namati (2014). The Nubians of Kenya. *Namati*. Available from: https://namati .exposure.co/the-nubians-of-kenya (accessed January 12, 2018).

Namati (2015). Justice and identity in Kibera. *Namati*. Available from: https:// namati.org/news/justice-identity-in-kibera/ (accessed January 12, 2018).

National Public Radio (NPR) (2018). For older voters, getting the right ID can be especially tough. *NPR*. Available from: www.npr.org/2018/09/07/ 644648955/for-older-voters-getting-the-right-id-can-be-especially-tough (accessed September 27, 2018).

Notimex (2015). Al menos dos millones de mexicanos en EU sin acta de nacimiento. *NTR*. Available from: http://ntrzacatecas.com/2015/04/21/al-menos-2-millones-de-mexicanos-en-eu-sin-acta-de-nacimiento/ (accessed October 1, 2018).

Nubian Rights Forum (NRF) (2018). *Outcomes of the 2016 NRF Mobile Birth Registration and School Outreach Program*, Nairobi: NRF.

Open Society Foundations (2010). *Dominicans of Haitian Descent and the Compromised Right to Nationality*, New York: Open Society Institute.

Open Society Justice Initiative (2011a). *Nationality and Discrimination: The Case of Kenyan Nubians*, Nairobi: Open Society Foundations. Available from: www.opensocietyfoundations.org/sites/default/files/kenyan-nubians-factsheet-20110412.pdf (accessed May 20, 2019).

Open Society Justice Initiative (2011b). *Nubians in Kenya: Numbers and Voices*, Nairobi: Open Society Foundations. Available from: www .opensocietyfoundations.org/sites/default/files/nubians-kenya-data-sheet -20110506_0.pdf (accessed May 20, 2019).

Open Society Justice Initiative, the Open Society Initiative for East Africa, Namati, and the Nubian Rights Forum. (2014). Briefing Paper: Implementation of Nubian Minors v. Kenya. Available from: https://www .opensocietyfoundations.org/sites/default/files/litigation-implementa tion-briefing-nubian-children-20170606.pdf (accessed May 20, 2019).

Ordoñez Bustamente, D. (2007). *El Subregistro de Nacimientos en Paraguay: Las consecuencias*, Washington, DC: Banco Interamericano de Desarrollo.

Ordóñez Bustamente, D. & Bracamonte Bardález, P. (2006). *El Registro de Nacimientos*, New York: Inter-American Development Bank.

Organization for Security and Co-operation in Europe (OSCE): Mission to Bosnia and Herzegovina (2005). *Report on the Roma Civil Registration Information Campaign*, Sarajevo: OSCE.

Pearce, K. (2017). Johns Hopkins volunteers help Baltimore ex-offenders acquire vital forms of ID. *Hub.* Available from: https://hub.jhu.edu/2017/02/13/identity-clinic-source/ (accessed January 29, 2019).

Pearson, S. J. (2015). Age ought to be a fact: the campaign against child labor and the rise of the birth certificate. *Journal of American History*, 101, 1144–1165.

Pero Ferreira, A. M. (2012). *Country Technical Note on Indigenous Peoples Issues: Republic of Paraguay*, Rome: International Fund for Agricultural Development.

Peters, B. G. & Mawson, A. (2016). *Governance and Policy Coordination: The Case of Birth Registration in Peru*, Florence: UNICEF Innocenti Research Centre.

Plan International (2004). *Situation Study and Basis for a Regional Programme for Supporting the Registration of the Birth of Children, Specialized Section (I): Dominican Republic*, Woking, UK: Plan International.

Plan International (2012). *Mother to Child: How Discrimination Prevents Women Registering the Birth of their Child*, Woking, UK: Plan International.

Plan International (2016). *Birth Registration for all in Indonesia: A Roadmap for Cooperation*, Woking, UK: Plan International.

Plan International & Coram International (2015). *Getting the Evidence: Asia Child Marriage Initiative*, Woking, UK: Plan International.

Plan International & UNICEF (2010). *Avances y desafíos para lograr el registro universal de nacimientos en los pueblos indígenas: Los casos de Bolivia, Ecuador, Guatemala, y Panamá*, Woking, UK, and New York: Plan International and UNICEF.

Platt, M. (2009). Not just a piece of paper. *Inside Indonesia.* Available from: www.insideindonesia.org/not-just-a-piece-of-paper (accessed October 29, 2018).

Price, P. J. (2013). Stateless in the United States: current reality and a future prediction. *Vanderbilt Journal of Transnational Law*, 46(443), 444–514.

Price, P. J. (2017). *Jus Soli* and Statelessness: A Comparative Perspective from the Americas. In B. N. Lawrance & J. Stevens, eds., *Citizenship in Question: Evidentiary Birthright and Statelessness*, Durham and London: Duke University Press, pp. 27–42.

Radiolab (2016). The girl who doesn't exist. *Radiolab.* Available from: www.wnycstudios.org/story/invisible-girl (accessed March 7, 2017).

Registro Nacional de Identificación y Estado Civil (RENIEC) (n.d.). Gestión Intercultural en el Registro Civil Bilingüe El RENIEC al rescate de las lenguas originarias del Perú. *RENIEC.* Available from: www.reniec.gob.pe/portal/html/registro-civil-bilingue/html/principal-rcb.jsp (accessed September 27, 2018).

Registro Nacional de Identificación y Estado Civil (RENIEC) (2012). *Plan Nacional Perú Contra la Indocumentación 2011–2015*, Lima: RENIEC.

Registro Nacional de Identificación y Estado Civil (RENIEC) (2015). Sigue creciendo el Registro Civil Bilingüe del Perú: Castellano – Aimara. *Revista Jilatxi*, 4, 1–60.

Reuben, W. & Carbonari, F. (2017). *Identification as a National Priority: The Unique Case of Peru*, Working Paper 454, Washington, DC: Center for Global Development.

Reuben, W. & Cuenca, R. (2009). *El estado de la indocumentación infantil en el Perú: Hallazgos y propuestas de politica*, Lima: World Bank.

Rice, S. E. & Patrick, S. (2008). Index of state weakness in the developing world. *Brookings*. Available from: www.brookings.edu/research/index-of-state-weakness-in-the-developing-world/ (accessed September 27, 2018).

Roca Serrano, E. (2006). *El Derecho a la Identidad en el Registro Civil de Bolivia*, Santa Cruz de la Sierra, Bolivia: Editorial Pais.

Rosenwaike, I. & Hill, M. E. (1996). The accuracy of age reporting among elderly African Americans. *Research on Aging*, 18, 310–324.

Ross, D. C. (2007). *Medicaid Documentation Requirement Disproportionately Harms Non Hispanics, New State Data Show*, Washington, DC: Center on Budget and Policy Priorities.

Rozzi, E. (2011). Undocumented Migrant and Roma Children in Italy: Between Rights Protection and Control. In J. Bhabha, ed., *Children without a State: a Global Human Rights Challenge*, Cambridge, MA: MIT Press, pp. 177–216.

Sadiq, K. (2008). *Paper Citizens: How Illegal Immigrants Acquire Citizenship in Developing Countries*, New York: Oxford University Press.

Scott, J. C. (1998). *Seeing like a State*, New Haven, CT: Yale University Press.

de Servin, Z. C. S. (2007). *Situación del registro de nacimientos en el Paraguay, según diversas fuentes*, Rome: Global Forum on Gender Statistics.

Shapiro, S. (1950). Development of birth registration and birth statistics in the United States. *Population Studies: A Journal of Demography*, 4(1), 86–111.

Simmons, B. (2009). *Mobilizing for Human Rights*, Cambridge, UK: Cambridge University Press.

Sing'oei, A. K. (2009). Promoting Citizenship in Kenya: The Nubian Case. In B. K. Blitz & M. Lynch, eds., *Statelessness and the Benefits of Citizenship: A Comparative Study*, Geneva: Geneva Academy of International Humanitarian Law and Human Rights and the International Observatory on Statelessness, pp. 38–50.

Stevens, J. (2017). Introduction. In B. N. Lawrance & J. Stevens, eds., *Citizenship in Question: Evidentiary Birthright and Statelessness*, Durham and London: Duke University Press, pp. 1–24.

Sugiyama, N. B. (2011). The diffusion of conditional cash transfer programs in the Americas. *Global Social Policy*, 11(2/3), 250–278.

Sumner, C. (2015a). *Indonesia's Missing Millions: Erasing Discrimination in Birth Certification in Indonesia*, Washington, DC: Center for Global Development.

Sumner, C. (2015b). Lessons from Indonesia's Missing Millions. In M. Castan & P. Gerber, eds., *Proof of Birth*, Sydney: Future Leaders, pp. 133–145.

UNHCR (2014). *Global Action Plan to End Statelessness: 2014–2024*, Geneva: UNHCR.

UNHCR (2017a). *This is our Home. Stateless Minorities and their Search for Citizenship*, Geneva: UNHCR.

UNHCR (2017b). *Ensuring Birth Registration for the Prevention of Statelessness*, Good Practices Paper, Action 7, Geneva: UNHCR.

UNICEF (2016a). *Birth Registration in Latin America and the Caribbean: Closing the Gaps*, New York: UNICEF.

UNICEF (2016b). *Health Equity Report. Analysis of Reproductive, Maternal, Newborn, Child and Adolescent Health Inequities in Latin America and the Caribbean to Inform Policymaking*, Panama City: UNICEF Latin American and Caribbean Regional Office.

UNICEF Indonesia (2014). A legal identity for all. *UNICEF*. Available from: http://unicefindonesia.blogspot.com/2014/10/a-legal-identity-for-all.html (accessed October 12, 2018).

UNICEF Innocenti Research Centre (2007). *Birth Registration and Armed Conflict*, Florence: UNICEF Innocenti Research Centre.

UNICEF Mexico & Instituto Nacional de Estadística y Geografía (n.d.). *Derecho a la identidad: la cobertura de registro de nacimientos en México en 1999 y 2009*, Mexico City: UNICEF Mexico.

United States Department of State: Bureau of Democracy, Human Rights and Labor (2015). Country reports on human rights practices for 2015 – Dominican Republic. *United States Department of State*. Available from: www.state.gov/documents/organization/253221.pdf (accessed February 11, 2019).

Valdés, L. M. (2011). Conmemoración del 150 aniversario del Registro Civil. Fundamentos y Reflexiones. Archived in the *Biblioteca Jurídica Virtual del Instituto de Investigaciones Jurídicas de la UNAM*. Available from: https://archivos.juridicas.unam.mx/www/bjv/libros/7/3067/3.pdf (accessed October 1, 2018).

Vengoechea Barrios, J. (2017). *Born in the Americas: The Promise and Practice of Nationality Laws in Brazil, Chile, and Colombia*, New York: Open Society Foundations, Open Society Justice Initiative.

de Verneuil, M. (2016). *Nationality: Romani; Citizenship: European*, Statelessness Working Paper Series No 2016/03, Eindhoven, the Netherlands: Institute for Statelessness and Inclusion.

Vidal Fuertes, C., Martinez, S., Celhay, P., & Claros Gómez, S. (2015). *Evaluación de Impacto, Programa de Salud Materno Infantil: Bono Juana Azurduy*, La Paz, Bolivia: Undiad de Análisis de Políticas Sociales y Económicos.

Visión Mundial Bolivia (2008). *Módulo Educativo: Construyendo Ciudadania*, La Paz, Bolivia: Visión Mundial Bolivia.

Westover, T. (2018). *Educated: A Memoir*, New York: Random House.

Wong, J. (2015). Achieving universal health coverage. *Bulletin of the World Health Organization*, 93, 663–664.

Wong, J., Skead, K., Marchese, A. *et al.* (2016). Reaching the hard to reach: a case study of birth registration in South Africa. *Reach Project*. Available from: https://issuu.com/reachproject/docs/south_africa_birth_registration (accessed September 27, 2018).

The World Bank (2017). 1.1 Billion 'Invisible' People without ID are Priority for new High Level Advisory Council on Identification for Development. Available from https://www.worldbank.org/en/news/press-release/2017/10/12/11-billion-invisible-people-without-id-are-priority-for-new-high-level-advisory-council-on-identification-for-development (accessed May 20, 2019).

World Vision International (2014). *Uncounted and Unreached: The Unseen Children Who Could be Saved by Better Data*, Federal Way, WA: World Vision International.

Acknowledgments

My debts in bringing this Element together are many and deep. I am enormously grateful to editors Ben Ross Schneider and Melanie Cammett for proposing the idea of a Cambridge Element on this topic, and for sponsoring a workshop at the Massachusetts Institute of Technology (MIT) that provided vital feedback on the ideas advanced here. I greatly appreciate the incisive comments that discussant Beth Simmons made at that event and the time she took to read the manuscript so carefully. Thanks also go to Jacqueline Bhabha and to Danny Hidalgo for their contributions to the discussion.

As always, I am grateful to my Latin Americanist colleagues at the University of Texas: Dan Brinks, Zach Elkins, Ken Greene, Raúl Madrid, and Kurt Weyland. Their extraordinary intelligence and erudition have inspired me and benefited my work for years. Thanks also go to Rob Moser, who, as department chair, has supported my research in multiple ways. I am also grateful to Paula Newberg, whose vast knowledge on many of the issues covered here has informed the project. I would also like to acknowledge Natasha Borges Sugiyama. The fieldwork we did together many years ago in Northeast Brazil first drew my attention to the problem of undocumented nationals.

I am privileged to have had three remarkable undergraduate research assistants whose work was crucial in bringing this project to fruition. Awesome in their talents and dedication were Amy Jeans, Michelle Martinez, and Francesca Reece. I am proud and humbled to have been their professor. Others to whom I am grateful for assistance on specific country cases include Tommy Burt, Fridah Mwendwa Kirimi, Faith Kwamboka Mariera, Luciana Molina, and José David Sierra Castillo.

To Andreas, Nikolas, and Kurt Weyland, I owe more than words can express. Their love and solidarity, and all the fun we have had together deep in the heart of Texas, power me on.

Cambridge Elements ≡

Politics of Development

Melani Cammett

Harvard University

Melani Cammett is Clarence Dillon Professor of International Affairs in the
Department of Government at Harvard University and Professor (secondary faculty
appointment) in the Department of Global Health and Population in the
Harvard T. H. Chan School of Public Health.

Ben Ross Schneider

Massachusetts Institute of Technology

Ben Ross Schneider is Ford International Professor of Political Science
at MIT and Director of the MIT-Brazil program.

Advisory Board

About the series

The Element Series *Politics of Development* provides important contributions on
both established and new topics on the politics and political economy of developing
countries. A particular priority is to give increased visibility to a dynamic and growing
body of social science research that examines the political and social determinants of
economic development, as well as the effects of different development models on
political and social outcomes.

Cambridge Elements ≡

Politics of Development

Elements in the Series

Developmental States
Stephan Haggard

Coercive Distribution
Michael Albertus, Sofia Fenner, and Dan Slater

Participation in Social Policy: Public Health in Comparative Perspective
Tulia G. Falleti and Santiago L. Cunial

CPSIA information can be obtained
at www.ICGtesting.com
Printed in the USA
LVHW021133220719
624835LV00007B/149/P